The Poor Side
of Town

The Poor Side of Town

And Why We Need It

HOWARD HUSOCK

Encounter
BOOKS
New York • London

First American edition published in 2021 by Encounter Books, an activity of Encounter for Culture and Education, Inc., a nonprofit, tax-exempt corporation. Encounter Books website address: www.encounterbooks.com

Manufactured in the United States and printed on acid-free paper. The paper used in this publication meets the minimum requirements of ANSI/NISO Z39.48–1992 (R 1997) (*Permanence of Paper*).

Portions of this work have appeared in *City Journal*, *New England Monthly*, *Commentary*, and the Winter 2021 issue of *National Affairs*.

FIRST AMERICAN EDITION

LIBRARY OF CONGRESS CATALOGING-IN-PUBLICATION DATA

Names: Husock, Howard, author.
Title: The Poor Side of Town: And Why We Need It / by Howard A. Husock.
Description: New York: Encounter Books, [2021] | Includes bibliographical references and index. | Provided by publisher.
Identifiers: LCCN 2021001391 (print) | LCCN 2021001392 (ebook)
ISBN 9781641772020 (hardcover; alk. paper) | ISBN 9781641772037 (ebook)
Subjects: LCSH: Low-income housing—United States—History. Public housing—United States—History. | Housing policy—United States—History. | Housing—United States—History.
Classification: LCC HD7287.96.U6 H87 2021 (print) | LCC HD7287.96.U6 (ebook) | DDC 363.5/969420973—dc23
LC record available at https://lccn.loc.gov/2021001391
LC ebook record available at https://lccn.loc.gov/2021001392

Interior page design and composition by Bruce Leckie

To my wife, Robin, and family

CONTENTS

The Neighborhoods We've Lost and the Ones We Need

A mong the greatest experiences of my life was serving in one of America's smallest political offices. For three terms during the 1980s, it was my honor to represent Precinct 6 at the Brookline, Massachusetts Town Meeting. In contrast to the classic New England "open" Town Meeting, which any adult resident may attend, ours was a "representative" version—a 240-member citizen legislature comprising 15 members from each of the 16 districts. All were volunteers. Yet our votes were consequential: We decided the annual budget appropriations for a municipality of nearly 60,000 people.

Debate could be intense. How much should go for the public schools, how much for the "town"—police and public works and more? (We called that the "town-school split.") Should the tax rate be raised? Should the long-standing ban on overnight street parking be relaxed, and should more rooming houses and bed-and-breakfasts be permitted? In a town that included both dense urban neighborhoods adjacent to Boston and postwar suburban areas, interests and issues ranged widely. Standing roll call votes could occur. There was no hiding for a Town Meeting member. During my tenure, the Town Meeting voted to phase out rent control—exposure to which helped move my own views from left to right. After I left, residents voted to permit the retail sale of marijuana. In other words, Town Meeting mattered.

As engaging and heated as such discussions could be—I won one election by a single vote— they were not, I now believe, the best aspect of this intense form of local democracy. What mattered more was what one would call the socioeconomic range of those gathering for several days at least twice annually in the high school auditorium to debate the "warrant articles" and to vote. During my time, the members included one of the most prominent geneticists in the world and the custodian at the Town Hall. There were always anti-war activists pushing for Town Meeting to pass resolutions condemning some military action—and the local American Legion leader resisting them and defending the tradition of saying the Pledge of Allegiance before sessions. White collar and blue collar, Black and white, Catholics, WASPs, and Jews, doctors and lawyers and firefighters and landscape architects.

This true diversity was not the result of some policy design. It was the natural result of the range of neighborhoods in Brookline. There was Pill Hill for the doctors, lined with historic Victorian-era mansions, and, at its bottom, the Point (formerly called Whiskey Point), historically Irish American and packed with two- and three-family frame homes. There were strongholds of New England Yankees—I think of the managing partner of a downtown law firm with colonial-era roots and the long-time chair of the important Town Meeting finance committee, which hashes out the annual budget before Town Meeting votes. There were the children of the blue-collar immigrant Irish, including the head of the Public Works Department union, who would become a major regional labor leader. There were middle-class Jews who'd made their way up and out of their Boston ghetto. (That would be me, if my extended family were included.) They lived in distinct neighborhoods but not at all far apart.

What was especially unusual, then, was this range of social classes working together in a shared civic polity. There were, to be sure, times when social class tensions flared, as when we debated funding for the public golf course, more likely to be used by "townies" than by the affluent members of private country clubs. (I didn't think we should be subsidizing golf for anyone!) But there was, without any doubt, a sense of common concern for all those who lived in the town. Among the best examples: the push to build a new school for those on the poor side of town. The drive to build the new William H. Lincoln elementary school to serve children of the Point was led by a scion of one of the oldest New England Yankee families and his wife, the head of the School Committee and an heir to a major American railroad fortune. (I was proud to serve as the Precinct 6 chair of the campaign.) Not only did the town decide to build the new school, which opened in 1994, but it hired one of America's most prominent architects, Graham Gund, to design it.

Our diverse polity was made possible by the town's range of housing types—and, in particular, the fact that it had what one used to call, unblinkingly, a poor side of town. There were districts and pockets of "three-deckers" with nicknames such as the Point, the Alley, and the Village. These neighborhoods were low-income but, historically, packed with corner stores, neighborhood schools, parish churches, good hockey players (including some Olympians), and working-class homeowners who rented to extended family members and friends. They had been built in the late nineteenth century by private developers such as the Brookline Land Company, which had assessed what the laborers and maids likely to occupy its homes could afford and built accordingly. It was what I like to call naturally occurring affordable housing.

But, beneath the relative comity of local democracy, there abided a dirty secret. The poor side of town had once been much bigger—hundreds of homes and dozens of blocks bigger. In the late 1950s and early 1960s, Brookline, imbued with the intoxicating progressivism of the times, had gone in big on federally subsidized urban renewal. That era's Town Meeting had voted to demolish what had come to be characterized as "slum housing."[1] Entire neighborhoods erected by the Brookline Land Company, known as the Farm and the Marsh, were torn down and their residents paid a nominal sum to move—including to newly built replacement public housing.[2, 3]

Cold water flats were replaced by modern high-rises—but gone were some 200 homes that the poor could afford, where small landlords knew their tenants. Gone were small businesses—an industrial laundry, auto body shops, and small "spas"—corner stores. There was some outcry in the neighborhood itself against such a course, but those voices were outnumbered. Nothing prevents a public housing tenant from running for Town Meeting, but, as a practical matter, it didn't happen. The tight social structure of low-income immigrant neighborhoods had helped local politicians emerge to protect local interests. That fell away. The fact that not all these poor neighborhoods were demolished allowed the mix that I savored to continue, but it was diminished. In the 1940s, the range of Town Meeting types had been even greater—lawyers and chauffeurs, doctors and laborers.

Brookline was, tragically, not exceptional in its treatment of neighborhoods built by private builders long before zoning laws and within the means of low-income families. A poor side of town—or, at least, a poorer side—was once the norm in America. Cities had their own low-income neighborhoods long before public housing, for which many of them were cleared. Notably, many of their inhabitants were African American. These neighborhoods—Bronzeville in Chicago, Black Bottom in Detroit, Desoto-Carr in St. Louis—shared many of the characteristics of Brookline's Farm: small homes with a significant number of local owners, small businesses, and their own influence on local politics. Even in the immediate period following World War II, suburban zoning was such that new, low-cost neighborhoods—affordable because of the large number of small homes close together—were able to spring up, including the most famous of them—Levittown, New York—as well as Skokie, north of Chicago, and my own hometown, South Euclid, Ohio.

But the formula for these "poor sides of town," or simple low-cost housing for the upwardly mobile, has somehow been lost. What can be called a kind of war on the poor sides of town was hardly confined to Brookline, long a progressive bastion. For decades, America has combined demolition and demonization of low-income neighborhoods with regulation and attitudes that impede their replacement. Two key factors have been at work. Zoning law proscribed the relatively modest density of small multifamily structures that makes housing naturally affordable—thanks to more homes on the same land area. At the same time, low-income housing has become synonymous with government-subsidized housing, including both the failed experiment of public housing and, more recently, efforts to disperse "affordable" (meaning government-subsidized) units into higher-income areas, said to be the antidote to public housing's problems. This has made for a deadly combination: limiting housing to larger lots, making it more expensive, and inspiring resistance in middle-class communities to subsidized rental housing, widely associated with lower-class households and the problems that developed in public housing.

This book tells the story of how this happened—from Jacob Riis's foundational exposé, *How the Other Half Lives*, and the

modernistic visions espoused by Catherine Bauer and imple-
mented by Robert Moses, to urban renewal and "exclusionary
zoning." It celebrates a historic alternative: neighborhoods of
modest homes—some very modest—many of them occupied
by owners and the basis not just for shelter but for deep neighborhood ties and a local politics that transcended the barriers of
social class. It promotes two goals: creating housing that those
of modest means can afford because of its sheer modesty, and
the restoration of neighborhood civil societies and local politics
shared by rich and poor. It argues that the time is right for a
back-to-the-future approach to housing that would achieve those
two complementary goals.

We need, in other words, a new version of the poor side of
town.

CHAPTER I

Jacob Riis and the Reformer's Gaze

The man who would do more than any other American to change the course of housing for the poor was not a builder or a tenant or a public health physician. Jacob Riis was a police reporter. But the man who would write *How the Other Half Lives* wasn't just any police reporter. Among the many competing on New York's Newspaper Row in the 1880s, he was, as his biographer Tom Buk-Swienty puts it, a "renowned police reporter," indefatigably following cops and health inspectors into the alleys of the Lower East Side, coming up with scoops crucial to the success of his paper, *The New York Tribune*.[1] The turning point of his career was a story about grave-robbing. He revealed that police had failed to come up with any leads in a sensational case of such body-snatching—a crime used to extort families desperate to get back the corpses of loved ones before they were sold to medical schools or doctors as cadavers. His reporting that police had no hope of solving the theft of the body of a department store magnate won him this accolade by a colleague: He had personally made "the *Tribune* police reports the best in the city."[2]

This is not just a footnote to the sources and methods Jacob Riis used for his landmark book about tenement life on New York's teeming Lower East Side in the late nineteenth century. It's crucial to understanding its contents and style—and its blind spots, the blinkered view that would lead to widespread antipathy toward the poor sides of town. Riis came of age professionally in the era of what would be called yellow journalism—urban mass media seeking to catch the eye of the casual reader. He was clear-eyed about what that took. "It was my task to cover all that news that means trouble to someone," he wrote.[3] That meant "deaths, accidents, crimes, fires, murders…epidemics…food-borne diseases.…Death and mayhem sold papers."

Stories that made Riis a top reporter included these: "The River's Unknown Dead"; "A Body Entirely Nude"; "Murder's Strange Tools"; "Ominous Signals (Fire Boxes Indicating Disaster and Death)." Riis specialized in writing about horrible suicides: the woman who, having lost her bank book, had thrown herself and her four children in front of a train. The man who soaked himself in lamp oil and set himself afire. Observes his biographer: "He mastered the genre to perfection."[4]

It was this formula that the onetime itinerant carpenter from Denmark would apply in the 1890 book that permanently secured his reputation and forever changed housing policy: *How the Other Half Lives: Studies among the Tenements of New York*. Why it became the bible of housing "reform" can be seen as the result of its series of powerful vignettes, such as its descriptions of back alleys where once-fashionable homes stood next to overcrowded tenement apartments:

Down the winding slope of Cherry Street—proud and fashionable Cherry Hill that was—their broad steps, sloping roofs, and dormer windows are easily made out; all the more easily for the contrast with the ugly barracks that elbow them right and left. These never had other design than to shelter, at as little outlay as possible, the greatest crowds out of which rent could be wrung. They were the bad after-thought of a heedless day. The years have brought to the old houses unhonored age, a querulous second childhood that is out of tune with the time, their tenants, the neighbors, and cries out against them and against you in fretful protest in every step on their rotten floors or squeaky stairs. Good cause have they for their fretting. This one, with its shabby front and poorly patched roof, what glowing firesides, what happy children may it once have owned? Heavy feet, too often with unsteady step, for the pot-house is next door—where is it not next door in these slums?—have worn away the brown-stone steps since; the broken columns at the door have rotted away at the base. Of the handsome cornice barely a trace is left. Dirt and desolation reign in the wide hallway, and danger lurks on the stairs. Rough pine boards fence off the roomy fire-places—where coal is bought by the pail at the rate of twelve dollars a ton these have no place. The arched gateway leads no longer to a shady bower on the banks of the rushing stream, inviting to daydreams with its gentle repose, but to a dark and nameless alley, shut in by high brick walls, cheerless as the lives of those they shelter. The wolf knocks loudly at the gate in the troubled dreams that come to this alley, echoes of the day's cares. A horde of dirty children play about the dripping hydrant, the only thing in the alley that thinks enough of its chance to make the most of it: it is the best it can do. These are the children of the tenements, the growing generation of the slums; this their home. From the great highway overhead, along which throbs the life-tide of two great cities [Manhattan and Brooklyn], one might drop a pebble into half a dozen such alleys.[5]

Riis's power lay in his ability to combine the sensational and the literary. His descriptions, like his crime reporting, were sure to appeal to the prurient interest of uptown readers who would themselves never venture to the "slums" but were fascinated by their decadence. It was of a piece with police reporting: the novelty of living conditions and situations readers could not imagine or experience for themselves, just as they could not imagine themselves as grave-robbers. That Cherry Street was once affluent only added to the horrible thrill.

But even such florid writing might not have changed American housing attitudes and policy were it not for an additional element, one that mattered above all: photographs. The onetime carpenter was fearless in experimenting with the chemistry that made possible a dramatic innovation: flash photography. Riis would use photography "showing, as no mere description could, the misery and vice he had noticed in his ten years of experience."[6] With the help of two colleagues, he carried his camera, his tripod, and the dangerous elements of a "pistol flash" to dark alleys and tenement interiors.

In effect, Riis was an early documentary filmmaker, memorably marrying narration and image: a little girl in a tenement hallway. A tenement apartment without windows. Children, forced to play in the street beneath clotheslines and amid shadows, who would have to sleep in the same rooms with adults of different sexes. The images were both powerful and poignant. Without them, it is impossible to imagine the outsized impact that *How the Other Half Lives* had.

Riis's reporting went further. It became the raw material of crusade. His reporting and images were complemented by what could be called early, amateur social science: documentation of the extent of crowding and disease, the prevalence of crime. There is reason to believe that Riis was outraged by what he saw and dedicated to changing it. At the same time, the marriage of shock and high-mindedness elevated the book. Readers could dwell, vicariously, in the pit of the Lower East Side, at the same time partaking in "muckraking" that might make the world a better place. After all, it was implied, no one should have to live in such conditions. That sentiment would lead Riis to the so-called "model tenement" movement toward more spacious, well-lit, and sanitary low-rent dwellings, made possible by benevolent investors willing to accept a below-market return on their capital. His was an early version of what would later be called stakeholder capitalism, or corporate shareholder responsibility. He knew, however, that such an approach was never going to be adequate to house the population of over a million people living on the Lower East Side. Still, it would set in place a thought formula that would serve as the essence of a housing reform movement: low-income neighborhoods built by ordinary builders were exploitative, overcrowded, and dangerous. Indeed, Riis even inspired an early instance of outright neighborhood clearance. After his book featured the infamous Mulberry Bend, said to be the most densely populated place in the world, it was torn down and replaced, in 1897, by a park, presaging latter-day urban "renewal."[7]

But, for all its length (some 300 pages) and the power of its images, there is one element of life on the Lower East Side that is stunningly absent from *How the Other Half Lives*: the voices of residents themselves. Riis seemed to have adopted the reformer's gaze and voice. He was the shocked, middle-class outsider, purveying upsetting images to others who occupied a similar place in the world. It presaged latter-day photography and film about war, famine, and refugees. How can people live like this? How can we permit them to live like this? Might their condition be a threat to our own? The reformer's gaze—like what later came to be called the cinematographic male gaze, which feminists would criticize—saw the Lower East Side from a specific but blinkered perspective. Riis and his reformist heirs saw neighborhoods in which they could not imagine living themselves, and thus concluded that these were places where no one should live.

Riis was building on the same views that were central to

the 1844 book *The Condition of the Working Class in England* by Friedrich Engels, later co-author with Karl Marx of the *Communist Manifesto*—but Engels's book, in comparison to that of Riis, suffered from its lack of photography, though not from a lack of political influence broadly. In it he stated, "The way in which the vast mass of the poor are treated by modern society is truly scandalous. They are herded into great cities where they breathe a fouler air than in the countryside which they have left."[8] Riis, in other words, overlooked a great deal—including, crucially, the fact that there were virtues in this vast poor side of town for those who had left pogroms, shtetls, and the subsistence farming of Ireland, Eastern Europe, and southern Italy behind. Their own view was not the bleak one implied by Riis. As Irving Howe would write of the same neighborhood Riis described, "Slowly, and at unmeasured cost, the immigrant Jews began to get a grip on their lives. By the mid-1890s, it had become clear that neither material suffering nor social uprooting would permanently break their morale, even if a good many were reduced to mute resignation. A determination to stick it out was, nevertheless, all but universal among the immigrants…the American idea had begun to take hold of the immigrant imagination.…A middle class, still fragile but increasing in numbers, started to make its appearance.…Poverty remained the basic condition, as it would for a good many years to come, but it was a poverty that took on a livelier complexion, a firmer tone."[9] Howe writes of immigrants who became shop owners, who became property owners themselves, who availed themselves of night school instruction in English, who moved up and out to other parts of New York.

His biographer Tom Buk-Swienty classed Riis among "reporters and writers who wrote about the slums focused primarily on suffering and squalor." In a biting critique of the reformer's gaze, Buk-Swienty, himself a Dane writing for a twenty-first–century Danish audience, was clear-eyed about Riis's limitations.

"In fact there was more to the slums than abject poverty. Hundreds of thousands of families lived relatively normal lives. They worked, although usually under deplorable conditions, paid rent, fed their children and had hopes and dreams for the future. For a large number of immigrants...life in the tenements was an improvement on their old lives, offering a more dignified existence." Crucially, he continued, in an insight that would remain elusive to subsequent generations of Riis-inspired housing reformers, "poverty was not a life sentence, as many writers, including Riis, at times, seemed to want readers to believe."[10]

Indeed, it would prove not to be—and poor sides of town, expanding but changing, would actually help in that process of upward mobility. "Even for tenement dwellers social mobility was possible...."[11]

CHAPTER II

The Zone of Emergence

There can be little doubt that *How the Other Half Lives* had a powerful and enduring impact. Its description of the use of backyard privies and poor sanitation was followed by a New York State law requiring cities to build public baths—and, in 1901, the first such facility opened on Rivington Street, on the Lower East Side. It had 91 showers and 10 baths—a sort of common-sense reform that, practically, sought to ameliorate, not eliminate, so-called slum conditions.[1] New York also passed the Tenement House Act of 1901, which, for the first time, required apartments to have outward-facing windows to let in both light and air.[2] Such "new law tenements" were understood as an improvement, but one that would not push rents entirely out of the reach of the poor (especially because "old law" tenements continued to operate).

Even the federal government, in an era before social legislation was the norm, became involved. In 1892, in the wake of Riis's exposé, Congress charged the office of the Commissioner of Labor (forerunner of the Department of Labor) with investigating slum conditions in cities with populations of more than 200,000. When that proved impractical, the charge was limited to New York, Chicago, Philadelphia, and Baltimore—cities that, in addition to New York, already spotlighted by Riis, were considered locations where the problems were most pronounced. The worst district in each city was selected, and the total number of people canvassed in the four districts was 83,852.[3]

This dramatically underappreciated investigation is a good starting point for countering the picture painted by Riis, to such long-lasting effect. "The results of the investigation," as a contemporaneous account put it, "are of a rather startling and unexpected nature."[4]

Yes, there were concentrations of saloons (Baltimore had the most, Philadelphia the fewest). Arrests were disproportionately high. But the overall picture as painted—and photographed—by Riis was called into question. "The unexpected statistics relate to earnings and health. The earnings in the slum districts are, as far as can be ascertained, quite up to the average earnings of workers generally; while the statistics show no greater sickness prevailing in the districts canvassed than in other parts of cities, and although sometimes in the most wretched conditions, a very small number of sick people were discovered." The police reporter had found the exceptions, not the norm. "Dr. Alfred Houghton, who was employed to test the sanitary condition of the atmosphere of the tenements, in his report states that the almost complete absence of pathogenic germs in the air of the slums is astonishing. The air in tenement houses was as pure as in any residence visited; the worst air was found in theatres.

"The exceedingly small proportion of persons sick during this year...is very noticeable."[5]

The neighborhoods, to be sure, in some ways fit the latter-day stereotype. As the slums investigation found, they were crowded with immigrants—they comprised 60 percent of the population of Philadelphia's slum district, for instance, and 40 percent of Baltimore's. They were poor Europeans: Italians, Russian Jews, Poles, Hungarians. And they were physically crowded. In Philadelphia, 12 percent of families lived in just one room. New York was actually less crowded: 44 percent of households lived in two rooms. The construction of the Williamsburg Bridge would pave the way for an exodus from the Lower East Side to the new attached houses of Brooklyn.

But the Bureau of Labor's investigation goes on to make clear that these teeming poor sides of cities were places where housing could be a key asset for upwardly mobile new Americans—and where the stereotypical absentee slumlord was far from universal. In Philadelphia, for instance, the growth of row houses—by 1920, the city would have no fewer than 299,000 such modest homes—made owner occupancy plausible, and an eye-popping 53 percent of slum households lived "in houses of one tenement, or in other words they occupy the whole house."[6] Riis's New York, where just 1.84 percent of slum households had a house to themselves, turned out to be exceptionally low compared to the other cities. Acolytes of Riis risked wrongly extrapolating from conditions on the Lower East Side to generalizations about low-income housing markets overall.

And residents could also be owners—or share a home with the owners.

In 1907, the United States Immigration Commission, which would be the next federal entity to examine the living conditions of poor immigrants, found that 30 percent of the poor took in lodgers.[7] To be sure, that could lead to crowding and shared bathrooms—but it also ensured that those renting out rooms would do their best to make sure a boarder would continue to rent and lodgers themselves would have to be on their best behavior. That's what one does when one needs income or a place to stay. One also may screen tenants—and evict those who fail to behave well. In these ways, not only is shelter provided but the social fabric is maintained. An economic relationship provides an incentive for limiting bad habits and bad behavior.

The extent of what I'm calling "owner presence"—an owner residing in his own home and/or renting rooms or apartments to others in the same structure—was notable. According to the 1894 Commissioner of Labor report, for instance, the slum district examined in Chicago had 73 owner-occupied two-family homes; 68 three-family homes; 51 four-family homes; and 48 five-family homes that were both owner- and tenant-occupied. This indicated that, because of the great many on-site rental units, a 10.2 percent rate of home ownership meant that 36 percent of households lived in the same residence as the owner (or were themselves owners). Of 3,881 total residential structures in the district of Chicago studied, 1,412 included units for both owner and tenants.[8]

This mattered in a number of ways. For the poor, home ownership represented, as it does for any household, a financial asset. That such an asset was income-producing due to rental units made it all the more valuable. Moreover, such a property served as an example; tenants could aspire to become owners and saw that possibility with their own eyes. In no small part because of Riis, the idea that the poor side of town was characterized mainly by absentee landlords would take hold in the reform imagination—but, in fact, New York was the exception in this regard, as noted above. Indeed, in his study of the development of Detroit in the early twentieth century, social historian Oliver Zunz found that, thanks to informal methods of construction and finance, "Working class immigrants owned their homes proportionately more often than middle-class, native white Americans....As a result of the high rate of home ownership and the plethora of single-family dwellings, only limited sections of Detroit resembled physical ghettos—downtown areas inhabited by minority group members who rented dilapidated homes from absentee owners."[9]

In their 1914 study of Boston immigrant neighborhoods, pioneer sociologists Robert Woods and Albert Kennedy observed that the ownership of modest properties—properties that the middle

SLUM HOUSING IN CHICAGO, 1894

Families and Individuals Living in Owned and in Rented Tenements Compared

Units in Structure	O/O	Renters	Total #	O/Presence
I	77	293	370	77
2	73	553	626	146
3	68	413	481	204
4	51	569	620	204
5	48	444	492	240
6	48	590	638	288
7	II	135	146	77
8	13	208	221	104
9	0	33	33	
10	I	18	19	10
11	3	26	29	33
12	0	48	48	0
13	I	14	15	13
14	2	25	27	27
15	I	31	32	15
18	0	18	18	0
22	0	24	24	0
24	0	42	42	0
TOTALS	397	3,484	3,881	1,412

OWNER-PRESENCE RATIO: 36 PERCENT

District Studied: Starting from Polk and Halsted Streets, along Halsted to Taylor, along Taylor to Newberry Avenue, along Newberry Avenue to Twelfth, along Twelfth to State, along State to Polk, and along Polk to Halsted.

classes of the day looked down upon—was crucial to the development of what they called "zones of emergence," that is, places where the immigrant poor joined the economic mainstream. Woods and Kennedy were key figures in the settlement house movement—they led the South End House in Boston—premised on the view that those of means had a responsibility to prepare poor newcomers to succeed in America. Their interest, in other words, was based not on Riis-like exposés of current conditions but on trends that would reflect that settlements were helping the poor rise. They found evidence of just that. They wrote that "nearly 50 percent of the small dwellings and three-family tenements are in the hands of onetime immigrant families in relatively humble circumstances. This real estate is mortgaged in a large share of its value but it stands as a symbol that the newcomers are 'taking possession of the land.'" Ownership of property is one of the surest indications that emergence is emergence, indeed.[10]"

They continued, almost poetically: "Over 65 percent of the residence property of the zone is owned by those who reside on it, and this is the best possible index that can be given of the end that holds the imagination and galvanizes the powers of a large proportion of the population. Doubtless the greater share of this property is encumbered with mortgage, but it is an index of striving and accomplishment."

Indeed, Woods, especially, saw the zones of emergence as linked to much more than housing—in many of the ways I would experience decades later in Brookline. As the prominent historian of urban neighborhoods Sam Bass Warner would put it in a preface to the 1962 edition of Woods and Kennedy's book—the first time it was actually made public, after having been discovered by a Harvard graduate student in neglected archives—"In the rise of families from slum conditions, and in the reorganization of slum community life, Woods saw the promise of urban democracy. In his view the voluntary associations of church and club must be revitalized, and the direct government institutions of the town meeting and the public school must become the models [for] urban regeneration through the creation of a metropolitan social structure of hundreds of democratic villages."[11]

The response of the private housing construction industry to the demand for modest dwellings was impressive. The first full-scale federal census of residential structures (1940) shows that between 1870 and 1940, the pre–public housing era, private builders were assiduously filling in the rungs of the housing ladder, building at strikingly high volumes—especially pre-Depression, particularly for the emerging urban working class. During that period in Philadelphia, no fewer than 299,000 attached, single-family row houses were built. In Brooklyn, more than 150,000 two-family homes were built, as well as 77,000 three-families and 45,000 one- to four-family structures with ground-floor store-fronts. In Boston, 21,000 three-family homes went up. Chicago, in 1940, had more than twice as many housing units in two-, three-, and four-family houses (382,028) as it had single-family homes (164,920).[12] "Two-flat" remains a common term in that city. These were both large absolute numbers and significant in terms of the percentage of population they represented. Boston's three-deckers, for instance, may have housed as much as a third of the city's pre–World War II population of 800,000, based on the somewhat generous assumption of an average of five persons in each three-decker unit.

Zones of emergence were developed even in California, with the construction of small bungalow-style homes on small lots. "The Roaring Twenties saw an explosion of house building in the East Bay. According to the Oakland Tribune Yearbook, 12,822 new homes were built in Oakland in just three years, 1921 to 1924, most of which were 'California Bungalows.' Prices were low. A four room Craftsman Bungalow built from a popular plan book could cost less than a thousand dollars. So popular was the California Bungalow that very few homes built in the 1920's were any other style."[13] Industrial Oakland, according to census data, also had significant numbers of two-, three-, and four-family homes.

Housing development in the U.S. before World War II offered sharply more variety than would later be the case. Even affluent suburbs incorporated many housing types. Shaker Heights, a Cleveland suburb once synonymous with great wealth, reflects its 1920s origins in its current housing types: 56 percent of units are detached single-family homes, and 20 percent are single-family attached houses or are found in two-unit structures (10.7 percent), three- or four-unit structures (2.3 percent), or five- to nine-unit structures (4.1 percent). The private developers who planned and built Shaker Heights understood that by building neighborhoods of smaller homes, they were including buyers who eventually might move up to larger ones.[14]

There were even some reform-minded voices who saw this trend and celebrated it, as in a 1911 paper for the National Housing Association—whose leader, Lawrence Veiller, would become the leading voice in the U.S. for local residential zoning and restrictionist anti-tenement building codes that would, in time, sharply limit the variety of America housing types and neighborhoods. The leader of the Association's Philadelphia chapter, Helen Parrish, however, held a distinct and constructive view, which she described as "one million people in small houses." Parrish particularly celebrated the boom in row-house construction in Philadelphia, which was providing widespread working-class owner occupancy. She prospectively disputed what would become the conventional idea that the private housing market inevitably failed those of modest means. "This plan of building can be made very successful financially; it fosters a conservative law-abiding spirit in the community, it gives even the smallest wage-earner an opportunity by thrift and economy to own a home; where he can conserve the best possible standard of family life." Parrish even captured, lovingly, what latter-day social scientists would call the social capital of neighborhoods built for those of modest means. "Fairs and festivals for the benefit of some church or charitable interest are often advertised in summer as being given by the people of some small street, each small house being decorated, and contributing its quota to the entertainment. Porch parties are frequently given." Parrish was the rare reformer who visited lower-income neighborhoods with an eye toward understanding them as their own residents did, who saw beyond the physical dimensions of homes and appreciated the lives of accomplishment she saw. (The row houses she celebrated typically had six rooms and a bath, far from spacious for a family with several children.)[15]

In contrast to later reformers, who were convinced that private markets could never serve those of modest means, Parrish wrote that row homes "are considered safe and profitable investments, and a builder who has proved himself conservative and intelligent in the use of capital has no difficulty in obtaining it."

Her emphasis on simply encouraging homebuilders to build more brings to mind the insights and observations of George Orwell in *The Road to Wigan Pier*, his narrative account of a mid-1930s trip through the industrial areas in the north of England. "For it is to be noted that the majority of these houses are old, fifty or sixty years old at least, and great numbers of them are by any ordinary standard not fit for human habitation. They go on being tenanted simply because there are no others to be had. And that is the central fact about housing in the industrial areas: not that the houses are poky and ugly, and insanitary and comfortless, or that they are distributed in incredibly filthy slums round belching foundries and stinking canals and slag-heaps that deluge them with sulphurous smoke—though all this is perfectly true—but simply that there are not enough houses to go round."[16]

But housing reformers, led by Riis acolyte Lawrence Veiller with the support of one of the first major American philanthropic foundations, the Russell Sage Foundation, were by no means agnostic about what sorts of new homes should be permitted to be built.[17] In his book *A Model Housing Law*—a proposal he traveled the country to promote to municipalities—Veiller provided a wealth of details about the extent of space, lavatories, and more. No detail was too small for what he termed "housing reform through legislation": "light and ventilation, intensive use of land, privacy, sewage disposal, egress in case of fire, improper use of cellars, providing receptacles of waste materials of all kinds...."[18]

Much of what Veiller proposed was unobjectionable—although it is one thing to push for fire safety and quite another to push for less intensive land use, which is itself the basis for making housing more expensive. Veiller would move on from housing law to become the pioneer of local zoning—limiting, by law, what types of buildings could be built in which locations. His early proposal for zoning law—later to be used as a cudgel against housing for those of modest means—was far from draconian. Residential homeowners would have to agree, block by block, to petition a municipality to zone the neighborhood as residential. Even then, one side of a street could continue to have commercial uses—stores, not stables (unless local owners agreed to such). It was assumed that two-family homes would be interspersed with single-family dwellings, providing the means for buyers who needed rental income to afford to become homeowners.

In other words, reform, up to this point, had yet to stand in the way of an up-and-out trend, from port of entry neighborhoods to new forms of homes for working-class families. The positive nature of the trend was even noted by reform contemporaries of Jacob Riis. Lillian Wald, the Lower East Side settlement house founder and pioneer public health nurse, was not shy about telling stories of hardship. But in her memoir, *The House on Henry Street*, she was clear-eyed about the long-term trend: "Through the tenements there is a stream of inflowing as well as outflowing life.... As our neighbors have prospered, many have moved to houses where they find better quarters, less congestion, more bathtubs...."

It would be the story told by the latter-day Tenement House Museum on the Lower East Side's Orchard Street that would celebrate "the urban log cabin"—a modest starting point for the upwardly mobile, not a dead end of degradation that demonstrated the evils of low-cost housing.[19] So, too, it's worth noting that the government did take steps to ameliorate living conditions; in addition to new tenement construction laws (regulation, not prohibition), in New York, noted Wald, "asphalt has replaced unclean, rough pavements; beautiful new school buildings (some the finest in the world) have been erected;...piers have been built for recreation purposes, and a chain of small free libraries of beautiful design." Such are the public goods (to use the economists' term) that an increasingly wealthy society owes its poor. The results were plain, observed Wald, who visited individual apartments on the Lower East Side and sought public health reforms, including safe milk, but was nonetheless alive to the good health of the neighborhood's good social character and the positive trajectory of the lives of residents. "Many times I have been impressed with the kindness, the patience, and sometimes the fortitude of our neighbors, and I have marveled that out of conditions distressing and nerve-destroying as these, so many children have emerged into fine manhood and womanhood...."[20]

A combination of private building and public investments was helping poor neighborhoods become better places to live, even as the poor themselves moved up and out. But a powerful countertrend, also born from the housing reform movement, was on the horizon—led by housing reform voices neither sympathetic to the growth of new forms of private housing for those of modest means nor, indeed, sympathetic to the immigrants occupying it.

Prescott Hall, a member of the same Boston elite that included Robert Woods and Albert Kennedy—cheering on immigrants as they moved up into the zone of emergence—was the head of the Brookline Civic League, an organization whose latter-day successor this author, who held views that had nothing in common with Hall's, would lead in the 1990s. More significantly, Hall was the founder of the Immigration Restriction League. He would have the ear of Massachusetts Senator Henry Cabot Lodge and greatly influence the federal Immigration Act of 1917.

The 1917 law asserted a federal framework for broadly restricting, rather than merely regulating, immigration. It imposed an $8 head tax on each arriving immigrant and froze out everyone from a huge swath of the globe known as the "Asiatic Barred Zone." It also expanded the list of prohibited "undesirables"—which already included epileptics, "imbeciles," and prostitutes—to encompass vagrants, alcoholics, a wider class of alien radicals, and the opaque "persons of constitutional psychopathic inferiority." Most important, and reflecting the centerpiece of Hall's argument, the law imposed a new literacy test that shut out any foreigners who lacked basic reading ability in their native language.[21]

Hall and his fellow Brahmin restrictionists celebrated the passage of the 1917 law with a quiet dinner at the Union Club on Boston's Beacon Hill. Far from being content, they were just getting started. Their efforts would have a more lasting payoff in subsequent years, culminating with a Draconian quota law signed by President Calvin Coolidge. A former governor of Massachusetts, Coolidge had lamented that the country was becoming a "dumping ground" and pledged that "America must remain American."[22]

Hall had a closely related housing agenda, as reflected in his 1917 essay "The Menace of the Three-Decker," published by Lawrence Veiller's National Housing Association journal, *Housing Betterment*.[23] The same structures that were to serve as rungs on a ladder of upward mobility in Woods and Kennedy's telling were abhorrent to Hall—who urged Massachusetts localities to bar them outright by prohibiting wooden walls in multifamily buildings. He celebrated the fact that new three-family homes had been limited to just four Massachusetts municipalities. They posed, he asserted, a fire risk and would, he was certain, be "prone to rapid deterioration." A century later, many of the homes Hall excoriated not only remain standing but are also expensive. They include those three-deckers that still stand in Hall's native town of Brookline—but, of course, not those hundreds in the Farm and the Marsh that were demolished just 40 years after Hall's essay. Housing reform was hitting home.

This was the shadow side of housing reform—one influenced by antipathy to new immigrants but having long-term implications, even as a tourniquet was placed on immigration.

CHAPTER III

"Modern Housing" and the Crusade Against the Poor Side

"They could have fixed it up. They didn't have to tear it all down."
——Frank Moroney, Massachusetts Democratic Party leader,
former resident, Brookline "Farm"[1]

"When I came to town, the people I lived with went to Bethel A.M.E. Church, which was located on Hastings and Napoleon. It's all torn away now. Just an expressway.... Negro businesses are just gone."
——M. Kelley Fritz, owner of a Detroit funeral home
in the "Black Bottom" neighborhood[2]

"Stood in Line at the County Hall/Heard the man saying we got some high-rise for y'all/Urban renewal/Negro removal."
——Detroit resident Aretha Franklin, in her
version of "Why I Sing the Blues"

"It is hereby declared to be the policy of the United States to alleviate the acute shortage of decent, safe and sanitary dwellings for families of low income."
——United States Housing Act of 1937

"There is little disagreement that housing constitutes one of the Nation's most serious economic and social problems today.... Over the years, we have never been able to produce enough housing at prices which a large proportion of the American people can afford."
——National Housing Act, 1949

Despite the combination of neighborhood improvements and upward mobility, the disdain for the poor sides of town initiated by Riis persisted and took hold, first intellectually, then in policy. A new generation of reformers would not acknowledge improvements. A slow-building wave would lead to a drastic change: outright demolition—"slum clearance"—of poor sides across the United States. They would be replaced with public housing—government-owned and -managed—and not to the benefit of the poor in whose interest it was ostensibly built.

The Riis reform gaze would be passed from the immigrant police reporter to others far more removed from the physical conditions of the poor sides of town. In his role as head of the National Better Housing Association, New York tenement reformer Lawrence Veiller pushed for what reformers celebrated as "restrictive" legislation, which dictated that houses it disapproved of should not be built. Over time, Veiller would become the key champion of city planning and zoning, aimed at dividing residential and industrial uses. Its implications for the development of modest neighborhoods would become far-reaching, but in the early twentieth century his efforts focused on tenement law.

But the most dramatic change in the fate of "slums"—existing low-income neighborhoods—would be their outright demolition and clearance. The crusade that culminated in that result was led by two American women, Columbia University faculty member Edith Elmer Wood and Vassar College graduate and Cornell University architecture student Catherine Bauer. Both were private school–educated members of the upper middle class, outraged by slum conditions and intent on a national program to ameliorate them through demolition and replacement.

The exposé-style reform made famous by Jacob Riis would be succeeded by a body of scholarly work—reform-focused social science that would not only continue to find slums to be without redeeming value but would pave the way for their widespread demolition. The idea that private, low-cost, low-income housing could be a way station to upward mobility was not considered by such observers as Edith Elmer Wood, who chaired the National Committee on Housing of the American Association of University Women.

In her 1934 paper "A Century of the Housing Problem" and a large body of other work, Wood led the charge that would, in part, guide New Deal housing policy against the private housing industry and against the idea that homeownership was an effective means for the poor to improve their station:

"The housing problem is an inevitable feature of our modern industrial civilization and does not tend to solve itself. Supply and demand do not reach it, because the cost of new housing and the distribution of income are such that approximately two thirds of the population cannot present an effective demand for new housing. And while some of the older housing is acceptable enough, a great deal is shockingly inadequate."[3]

Wood must be considered a key successor to Riis in the war against poor sides of town. In her view, however, the poor were to be housed—indeed, had a right to housing—but building homes for those with low incomes would have to be the task of government. In "A Century of the Housing Problem," she acknowledged that Philadelphia should be "justly proud" of its owner-occupied row houses—but such success did not lead her away from the ambitious vision that would become known as public housing.

"There are housing conditions all over the United States which cannot be tolerated in civilized communities. Restrictive housing laws, energetically enforced, ameliorate bad conditions but cannot cure them. Model housing enterprises, of philanthropic or industrial origin, neither do nor ought to supply the demand.

"How then is the problem to be solved?"

The answer would be apartment blocks built and managed by government authorities: public housing.

Tenement reform legislation had raised the cost of apartment construction—leading to the conclusion that the private market would inevitably fail a large portion of the population and that the government must step in as the builder of first resort.

But public housing would not just provide new housing for the poor. It would replace the poor sides of town—which would be demolished outright. The clearance would include not only residential structures but businesses and community institutions. Superficially, the erection of public housing might be seen as a means of bringing safe and sanitary housing within the financial range of that part of the population for whom it was out of reach.

But the change was far greater. It meant that the intricate networks of poor neighborhoods—owners renting to tenants they knew and boarders they took in; small stores on ground floors or next door; churches and mutual aid organizations—this self-organized world was to be swept away based on the vision of reformers who were distant from and uninvolved in the poor sides of towns, who never lived in these neighborhoods or consulted with their residents. Swept away were not just physical structures, about which one might have varying views, but the dense set of relationships that would later be called social capital and civil society—accumulated by those who were in it together, based on their shared station in life and aspirations of improvement. It is not too great a stretch to argue that as African Americans moved from Southern farms to Northern cities, they were in effect following the self-improvement path trod by previous waves of European immigrants, accumulating property and commercial assets based in an ethnic neighborhood of their own. This process was harshly interrupted by housing reform. Ownership was replaced by bureaucracy, neighborhoods subsumed in institutional life.

One key to understanding what was lost is a statistic not widely considered when examining the quality of life in "slums," and that I have referred to as owner presence. It's a way to understand not just how many homes were occupied by their owners but also how many other units were rented in structures where the owner lived. Again, think of a two- or three-family home in which the owner lived on one floor and rented out the others.

I became aware of the Irish American neighborhood called the Farm as a Town Meeting member who had to vote to approve the ongoing costs of Brookline's Redevelopment Authority there. Town records made it possible to calculate owner presence in this lost community even though census data from the era is not yet available. Multifamily structures—particularly New England "three-decker" frame houses—were common, constructed beginning in the mid-nineteenth century, unconstrained by zoning law. The 121 homes in the Farm had 348 units. More than half were occupied by either an owner or a tenant whose owner lived in the same house.[4] Keep in mind that, in the public housing that replaced the Farm, there is, by definition, zero private ownership. And in recent years, frame three-family homes in generally affluent Brookline have become highly valuable, typically selling for well north of a million dollars. Although Farm owners were modestly compensated, they missed out on the asset appreciation realized by other parts of Brookline, such as the neighborhood I represented.

A review of census data for parts of Chicago, Detroit, Cleveland, and St. Louis that were cleared to make way for public housing tells a similar story. In Chicago, 32 percent of structures in areas that would later be cleared for public housing were owner-occupied; in Detroit, 29 percent; in Cleveland, 49 percent; in St. Louis, 38 percent. In two all-Black census tracts in that city, 21 percent of properties (828 homes) were held by non-white owners, but there were only 721 single-family structures.[5]

Such neighborhoods would have qualified as areas of concentrated poverty, yet had significant positive aspects, as manifested notably by homeownership rates. In 1950, St. Louis was a city with 856,796 people, 702,348 of whom were white (about 82 percent) and 153,755 of whom were Black (about 18 percent). The median income was $2,718 in 1950 (about $30,000 in 2021 dollars).[6]

An examination of two nearly all-Black neighborhoods based on 1950 U.S. Census data disproves the claim that absentee slumlords controlled much of the real estate and bilked tenants. The proportions of owner-occupied buildings for both neighborhoods were below the citywide average—34 percent owner-occupied and 41 percent of structures with an owner present—although not by much. For instance, census tract 11-A, which I call Northside A, was 98 percent Black, and 21 percent of all housing units (828 of 3,696) were owned by non-whites, most likely Blacks; at least a quarter of these units were occupied by their owners. Interestingly, the proportion of owner occupants (21 percent) in this particular census tract exceeds that of an adjacent, predominantly white census tract (18 percent). In contrast, census tract 21-B, which I call Northside B, was 96 percent Black, and most of the units were owned by non-whites (95.8 percent, 460 out of 480), and at least 23 percent of all housing units had an owner occupier.

In Northside A, Northside B, and the predominantly white census tract adjacent to Northside B, rents ($27.71, $21.85, and $17.53 per month in 1950 dollars, respectively) were lower than the citywide median ($28.55) and the predominantly white census tract adjacent to Northside A ($33). Not surprisingly, the housing quality in Northside A and B was low. For example, in Northside A, Northside B, and the predominantly white census tract adjacent to Northside B, 30, 56, and 44 percent of the housing stock, respectively, did not have a private bath or were deemed dilapidated, compared with 28 and 30 percent of the housing stock citywide and in the predominantly white census tract adjacent to Northside A, respectively. In sum, there were poor Black as well as white census tracts in St. Louis in 1950. The preceding refutes the conventional tale that, historically, low-income housing was chiefly provided by slumlords—absentee landlords who took advantage of the limited housing opportunities available to the poor to reap outsized profits.

"Owner presence," in other words, was notably higher in "slums" than in individual units that were owner-occupied. The landlord, let's say, lived upstairs—maybe two floors up. Maybe the landlord was an uncle or a grandmother who babysat. Owner occupancy created the potential for an even greater dimension of owner presence. Both were kernels of upward mobility and accumulation of wealth that were wiped out. Data from the 1950 federal census tells the story.

CHICAGO (1950)

ALL CENSUS TRACKS AVERAGE

13.4 percent Black   33.3 percent owner-occupied (among census tracks 60 percent or more Black: 14.4 percent owner-occupied)

CENSUS TRACK AVERAGE WHERE PUBLIC HOUSING WAS BUILT

64 percent Black   16 percent owner-occupied

CLEVELAND (1950)

ALL CENSUS TRACKS AVERAGE

15.3 percent Black   41.3 percent owner-occupied (among census tracks 60 percent or more Black: 18.9 percent owner-occupied)

CENSUS TRACK AVERAGE WHERE PUBLIC HOUSING WAS BUILT

21.9 percent Black   32 percent owner-occupied

DETROIT (1950)

ALL CENSUS TRACKS AVERAGE

14.9 percent Black   52.5 percent owner-occupied (among census
                      tracks 60 percent or more Black: 28.1 percent
                      owner-occupied)

CENSUS TRACK AVERAGE WHERE PUBLIC HOUSING WAS BUILT

35.7 percent Black   10.3 percent owner-occupied

ST. LOUIS (1950)

ALL CENSUS TRACKS AVERAGE

12.5 percent Black   39.4 percent owner-occupied (among census
                      tracks 60 percent or more Black: 15.1 percent
                      owner-occupied)

CENSUS TRACK AVERAGE WHERE PUBLIC HOUSING WAS BUILT

56.1 percent Black   7.6 percent owner-occupied[7]

One could argue that public housing was needed to upgrade so-called slum conditions. However, that argument rests on the assumption that less-than-ideal physical conditions should be the main gauge of the health of a community, and that demolition and redevelopment are the only options available to improve matters. In reality, it substituted for the option of transforming neighborhood residents into homeowners, the traditional mechanism for providing economic improvement for Americans. In other words, we must be cautious in assuming that policy can be designed to definitively increase the likelihood of household upward mobility and that we can ascertain what the social and environmental preconditions for upward mobility actually are.

The sociologist Nathan Glazer reflected the evolution of his own views from favoring "modern housing" to deep skepticism about it. In 2007, Glazer, who had served briefly in a federal housing agency in the early 1960s, published *From a Cause to a*

Style: Modernist Architecture's Encounter with the American City.
Modernist buildings began as a utopian cause, Glazer pointed
out—indeed, as social policy crafted by technocratic elites for
the benefit of the working class. Glazer candidly recalls seeing
a photo of a dozen blocks of tenements that had been razed to
make way for housing projects: "I recall, as a social-minded,
and socialist, youth, looking at this picture, proud at what had
been done, worried about how long it would take to clear away
the surrounding sea of slums." But those tenements that sur-
vived, he continues, "are now often more desirable not only to
poor people but to middle-class people too." Glazer cites the
East Harlem brownstones of his youth: "No one has ever had a
good word for this nondesign, this simple adaptation to market
needs—until we started destroying it. Then we discovered that
the brownstones could provide good living quarters...that the
tenements, once the severe overcrowding was remedied...also
provided good living space."[8]

This is important for a range of reasons. Homes that were
condemned may not have been in ideal physical condition, but
they were economic assets occupied, in many cases, by their
owners. As the sociologist Michael Ullman has observed, in an
unpublished manuscript shared with the author, those owners,
and even their tenants, had the option to rent rooms to boarders
or extended family members in order to make ends meet. This is
not, Ullman astutely observes, an option in public or otherwise
subsidized housing. (He links the rules meant to limit overcrowding to the later increase in family homelessness and the rise in
the family shelter population.)

These neighborhoods were also home to employers, including businesses both large and small. In the Mill Valley section of
St. Louis, which was later cleared, the Dixie Cream Donut Flour
building was within walking distance of a dense residential area.[9]
In Brookline's Farm, onetime residents recall neighbors who

worked at an industrial laundry. In Detroit's Black Bottom, the Urban League was especially active, helping rural newcomers find places to live and adjust to city life.

These clusters of small homes, small businesses, churches, and mutual aid organizations were swept away by reformers, who showed no appreciation for this mix of residential employment and social purposes. Nor did they show much concern for the opinions of those they were trying to help. As Peter Rossi and Robert Dentler wrote in their book on urban renewal in Chicago, *The Politics of Urban Renewal*, proponents of the idea actually faced opposition from those whose neighborhood was ostensibly to be upgraded. "The community was viewed by Negroes as an almost ideal residential location far from blighted or deteriorated. For Negroes from every class level…the importance ascribed by whites to renewal seemed only a flimsy excuse. Except at the uppermost level of the Negro community, renewal plans were seen as directed specifically against Negroes" and a stalking horse to create middle-class housing for whites.[10] That, indeed, is what happened to portions of Black Bottom: Once cleared, it became the site of an upscale apartment complex called Lafayette Park, designed by the modernist architect Mies van der Rohe.[11]

That public policy could have come to such a pass says much about the housing reform gaze. Edith Elmer Wood, the theoretician of public housing, lived a life distant from any sort of subtle understanding of what she blithely dismissed as slums. Raised in Portsmouth, New Hampshire, she was the daughter of a Navy officer, graduated from Smith College, and later received a doctorate from Columbia. Prior to her career as a reformer, she aspired to be a short-story writer and published a set of romance short stories about boarding school girls, collected in an anthology entitled *Shoulder-Straps and Sun-Bonnets*. She brought the confidence of the upper class to her reform proposals. "Housing of its unskilled workers is America's next great problem," she wrote in 1918, even as the construction of a great range of modest housing types was well underway and the country stood on the edge of a decade of great prosperity.[12] "Our national future will be one of progress or decadence according to the way in which we handle it. Never again shall we go back to the laissez-faire attitude—nor should we wish to." Like latter-day reformers, she invoked the cause of children to emotionalize her proposals to give governments the tools to build—or to restrict—housing. "No other single agency—not even the baby clinic or the public school—exerts such an influence for good or evil as the home that forms the baby's almost exclusive environment."[13] One can only wonder what she would have thought about the lives of those raised in the pre–public housing Lower East Side who went on to win the Nobel Prize (Rosalyn Yalow, mathematics; Isador Isaac Rabi, physics) or be judged by the American Film Institute as one of America's greatest movie actors (Edward G. Robinson). Indeed, there would come a time when a Lower East Side apartment would be converted into the Tenement House Museum in recognition that such slum housing served as America's "urban log cabin"—the first step toward later success.[14]

If Wood provided the theory, another woman housing reformer would provide the blueprints. Catherine Bauer attended the private Vail-Deane School in her hometown of Elizabeth, New Jersey, where her father was an early highway engineer. (Joseph Bauer is credited with designing the first highway cloverleaf exchange.) She graduated from Vassar, attended Cornell architecture school, and then lived in Paris, becoming part of a group of modernist artists and architects that included the photographer and painter Man Ray and the architect Fernand Leger. In the late 1920s, she was living a bohemian life in Greenwich Village before work in publishing drew her toward housing reform. The critic Lewis Mumford would introduce her to the work of the ultimate modernist, the Swiss architect Le Corbusier, whose high-rise "workers' housing," set on campuses without streets—later known as "towers in the park"—had begun to sprout in the Paris suburbs. She and Mumford toured Europe in 1932 to observe the new housing projects in France and Germany; later, with support from the Carnegie Foundation, she did the same in the USSR. Their joint work was published in *Fortune* magazine and informed a landmark 1932 exhibit at New York's Museum of Modern Art, for which Bauer wrote the text to accompany photos and drawings of European "social housing."

When New York began to build its public housing system, by far the nation's largest, it made two ill-fated decisions: not only would the city demolish existing working-class "poor side" neighborhoods; it would also put into practice the modernist vision of towers-in-the-park architecture. The dynamism of the city—its small blocks and diverse residential building types, its buffet of shops and stores—was to be swept away.

"The plan must rule," Le Corbusier decreed, and in his designs, it did. "There ought not to be such things as streets," he wrote. "We have to create something that will replace them."[15] That something was the superblock.

Bauer was enthralled with both modernist architecture and the idea that it should replace existing low-rent housing. Her vision was that of a modernist worker's housing utopia—and would have an outsized influence in pushing the United States in that direction. Photography and architecture would both play major roles in Bauer's profoundly influential 1934 book *Modern Housing*. But her written message was even stronger than Abbott's. "The need to remove housing from private hands was the principal message of *Modern Housing*," writes architectural historian Barbara Penney in the forward to a 2020 edition of that book. Frank Lloyd Wright, who liked Bauer personally, called her "Communist Catherine." Wrote Bauer, admittedly in the depths of the Depression, when housing construction of all kinds was at a standstill: "There is no getting around the fact that modern housing and much of the framework of contemporary Western society are mutually antipathetic. The premises underlying the most successful and forward-pointing housing developments are not the premises of capitalism, of inviolate private property, of entrenched nationalism, of class distinction...."[16] Not only the physical conditions but the very idea of a poor side of town was anathema to Bauer—who believed that private construction would fail to provide decent housing for up to two-thirds of the public, echoing Wood.

Modern Housing specifically promoted the Le Corbusier–style social housing in Europe as the more advanced approach to housing policy that the U.S. should adopt. Indeed, Bauer explicitly cited Le Corbusier's utopian high-rise vision of his 1923 Cities of Tomorrow, which itself would transform the outer edges of many European cities and earned him an invitation to the Soviet Union to assist in the architectural transformation of Moscow. *Modern Housing* was replete with rotogravure photographs of such projects, including and admiringly the housing blocks of the Soviet Union. (Le Corbusier, in practice, became disillusioned with Stalin.)[17]

In reality, these Soviet model housing blocks were far from typical. Even as the private housing market's "zone of emergence" was providing tens of thousands of small homes for formerly very low-income households, the socialist model was actually stuck in what, for the U.S., was quickly becoming the housing past. A historic study commissioned by the U.S. Central Intelligence Agency would later find typical living space in Soviet post-revolutionary housing comprised just "6.5 square metres (70 square feet) per person, or less than three-quarters of the minimum sanitary norm. In other words, every dwelling consisting of two rooms was inhabited by five people; thus between two and three people had to share one and the same room all the time."[18]

Just a year after *Modern Housing* was published, the Roosevelt Administration, which both Wood and Abbott joined, began breaking ground on U.S. public housing. "First Lady Eleanor Roosevelt turned up on Sept. 7, 1935 for the groundbreaking [in Detroit]. And when Brewster homes opened in 1938, they became America's first public housing project built for African Americans."[19] This would prove to be more a curse than a blessing. In what must have seemed to her benevolent Progressivism, Mrs. Roosevelt had personally pushed for public housing projects to include Blacks. By that time, Bauer had taken a position in the Administration and had authored the landmark National Housing Act of 1937, which would become the basis for all government-subsidized housing in the U.S.[20] The Brewster Homes would physically replace acres of Detroit's Black Bottom, the historic Black neighborhood bordered by the famous combination residential and entertainment district known as Paradise Valley. Public housing would not be built on green fields; it would be the rationale used to clear poor sides of town and replace them with modernist structures assumed to offer a healthier physical and social environment.

What was lost continues to be remembered by Black Detroiters. Indeed, a project called the Black Bottom Archives was founded in 2015 to record oral histories of surviving residents, mount photographic exhibits, and tell the story of the neighborhood's demolition. Co-founder P.G. Watkins notes that, when started, the project was using the Black Bottom name somewhat symbolically, as a way to signal a project that was to focus on a history of what Watkins calls "disinvestment" in Black Detroit neighborhoods. But the idea of remembering Black Bottom itself proved to exert a hold on the imaginations of Black Detroiters. Says Watkins: "It was a place with hundreds of black-owned businesses, of black property owners, where there were black pharmacists, doctors and lawyers, historic churches and all kinds of mutual aid."[21] The memory of it lingers to the point that a local Detroit historian offers guided walking tours of what little remains, describing Black Bottom as an "economic and residential center."[22] It was cleared and landowners were minimally compensated for what was considered low-value land, just as Detroit was poised, at least during the 1950s, to become a boom town.

The demolition of thriving African American neighborhoods can seem shocking in retrospect. As one Detroit history puts it: "Hastings Street, which ran north-south through Black Bottom, had been a center of Eastern European Jewish settlement before World War I, but by the 1950s, migration transformed the strip into one of the city's major African-American communities of black-owned business, social institutions and night clubs. It became nationally famous for its music scene: Major blues singers, big bands, and jazz artists—such as Duke Ellington, Billy Eckstine, Pearl Bailey, Ella Fitzgerald, and Count Basie—regularly performed in the bars and clubs of Paradise Valley entertainment district. It is also where Aretha Franklin's father, the Reverend C.L. Franklin, first opened his New Bethel Baptist Church on Hastings Street."[23]

The fact that the replacement "projects" were racially segregated was not a concern for that era's reformers; Eleanor Roosevelt worked to make sure that the program would include Blacks. But once they were, it was clear that Blacks would be directed to their own projects. As Richard Rothstein wrote of the earliest New Deal public housing, sponsored by the Public Works Administration headed by Roosevelt Brain Trust member Harold Ickes, "The housing that the PWA built was always segregated, and it nearly always helped make existing neighborhoods more segregated than they were before."[24] Ironically, a Chicago public housing project named for Ickes became notorious as a hub of gang activity and was eventually demolished.[25]

The Brewster Homes (later Brewster-Douglass Homes) and

the demolition of Black Bottom would be the prelude to similar projects in Chicago, Boston, St. Louis, Cleveland, and most of all New York, where the public housing system would eventually comprise more than 170,000 apartments. Slum clearance was the predicate for most, as not just the poorest but working class and urban neighborhoods, and even their street names, were wiped off the map. It simply never occurred to the reformer that, as the sociologist Nathan Glazer would write of the residents of Boston's West End—another tenement neighborhood cleared, like Black Bottom, for middle-class housing—some people might prefer "low-rent to status" when they lived in areas whose "status as slums was open to doubt."[26] As Herbert Gans would write in his account of the West End, *The Urban Villagers*, a focus on physical standards had "so far failed to make a distinction between low-rent and slum housing.... Slums should be eliminated but low-rent structures must be maintained, at least in the absence of better housing for people who want, or for economic reasons must maintain, low rental payments and who are willing to accept high density, lack of modernity and other inconveniences as alternative costs."[27] One can only wonder whether Gans felt constrained to write that slums should be cleared—and whether he saw any real distinction between what some called slums and others simply called a low-rent neighborhood.

One cannot overstate the irony of public housing in practice, in contrast to its theory. Benign management, with no interest in profit, was to administer housing maintained by its own stream of rental income. But that income would prove inadequate as the projects aged and complexes named for prominent African American progressives—Frederick Douglass, the anti-lynching advocate Ida B. Wells, the poets Langston Hughes and James Weldon Johnson—became what a euphemistic federal report would later term "severely distressed." A latter-day Jacob Riis could not help but find the abject conditions that concerned him in the public housing meant to replace such conditions. A program explicitly intended to create a healthy environment for children provided, in many places, anything but. Indeed, the journalist Alex Kotlowitz titled his gripping and tragic account of the dangers of life at Chicago's Henry Horner Homes, named for a one-time Illinois governor, *There Are No Children Here.*[28]

Even Catherine Bauer herself, not that many years after the publication of *Modern Housing*, recognized that the program was not going well. In her 1957 essay "The Dreary Deadlock of Public Housing," published in *Architectural Forum*, she "found little to praise in the program, as it had evolved." Rather, she saw "rigidity and paternalism in management, crudity and segregation in project design."[29]

But it was in 1971 that there was a quintessential demonstration that the public housing substitute for the poor side of town had failed. The Pruitt-Igoe public housing project of St. Louis, built and first occupied between 1954 and 1956, was modern housing par excellence. It had been built on the cleared DeSoto-Carr neighborhood, which, like its counterparts in Detroit, had aspects of the abject but also included significant elements of owner presence and commercial enterprises. The cleared space became the blank slate for the drawing board of a premier international modernist architect, Minoru Yamasaki, who would also design Lower Manhattan's World Trade Center Towers, which fell on September 11, 2001. Pruitt-Igoe's 57-acre site comprised 33 11-story buildings, praised by *Architectural Forum* as "slum surgery" and "the best high apartment of the year."[30] By 1970, it had become the subject of sociologist Lee Rainwater's tellingly titled book *Behind Ghetto Walls: Black Life in a Federal Slum.*

"Pruitt-Igoe houses families for which society seems to have no other place. The original tenants were drawn from several land clearance sites in the inner city. Although there were originally some white tenants, all of the whites have moved out and the population is now all Negro. Only those Negroes who are desperate for housing are willing to live in Pruitt-Igoe—over half the households are headed by women; over half derive their household income from public assistance of one kind or another." A questionnaire that a research team headed by Rainwater distributed found the following responses were common: "There's too much broken glass and trash outside; the elevators are dangerous; the elevators only stop at every other floor so people have to walk up or down to get to their apartments; there are mice and cockroaches in the buildings; people use the elevators and halls to go to the bathroom. Little children hear bad language all the time so they don't realize how bad it is. The laundry rooms aren't safe. Clothes get stolen and people are attacked.

"Pruitt-Igoe condenses into one 57-acre tract all the problems of race and poverty."[31]

Rainwater, the flat language of social science notwithstanding, was a latter-day Riis describing housing that was built to replace the sort of neighborhoods described in *How the Other Half Lives*—except these were conceived by leading experts and designed by leading architects at government expense. Pruitt-Igoe was not just another housing project but was quintessential "modern housing," designed to replace Black communities judged to be irredeemable slums.

Yet in 1971, after Pruitt-Igoe had not even stood for two decades, its demolition by spectacular implosion began—and the project became synonymous with the failure of public housing in practice. The poor side of town had been replaced with something far worse: a place where a distant and dysfunctional management had supplanted dispersed ownership; where streets lined with stores and churches were replaced by large, windswept campuses that would become spaces residents feared to cross; where walk-up buildings were replaced with towers in which the elevators failed and stairways became havens for criminals. This was supposed to have been the modernist's dream, the environment in which children would thrive—planned by visionaries. Instead, it was a place of the sort Jane Jacobs described as being shaped by "nobody's plans but the planners," who thought they could design the basis for daily life. The African American sociologist Joyce Ladner, who studied Pruitt-Igoe, compared it unfavorably with her own childhood home in shack-ridden Jim Crow Mississippi. Ladner observed the project as a young academic and notes the similarity of the Pruitt-Igoe population to that with which she had grown up in Mississippi. Its racial segregation made it similar "except for one thing: The strong, tightly knit communities and families in which I'd grown up had begun to shatter around the people who were displaced in a northern city with few supports."[32]

Sadly, the collapse of the dream of Abbott and Bauer would not prompt the rethinking it suggests—a return to permitting poor sides of town to arise, knowing that, in a far richer America, they would not likely take the same form as that which Riis decried. Instead, a search for a public housing philosopher's stone, a magic formula, would continue. But it would do so as a tragic sideshow to a wave of private American housing construction that began after World War II—one that included what can well be viewed as a new version of the poor sides of towns.

THE DESTRUCTION OF BLACK BOTTOM

Detroit's Black Bottom neighborhood provides the perfect prism through which to see the unfortunate ways in which public housing and its close cousin, urban renewal, destroyed African American institutions and robbed residents of the chance to accumulate wealth. It's a story well told by historian Jamon Jordan, the president of the Detroit chapter of the Association for the Study of African American Life and History.

Increased appreciation for what was lost when Black Bottom was cleared has led the onetime middle school social studies teacher to a new career as a tour guide for university and high school groups interested in the handful of buildings—including public schools—that remain of what was once a dynamic community of 130,000, replete with more than 300 Black-owned businesses.

Jordan is quick to note that the name Black Bottom was not racially inspired. The early French settlers of Detroit had noted its rich black soil. He is quick to note, as well, that it was housing segregation that played a key part in the formation of Black Bottom as an African American neighborhood in the first place. Blacks—who had first settled in the area during the Underground Railway era—had limited choices as to which neighborhoods they could move into during the time of the so-called Great Migration from the South, from the 1920s through the 1940s. It was, notes Jordan, an era in which private deed restrictions still commonly barred the sale or rental of homes to Blacks. (These were not declared unconstitutional by the Supreme Court until 1948.)[33]

He is clear-eyed in acknowledging the crowding in both Black Bottom and the adjoining, also Black, Paradise Valley neighborhood, as well as the fact that some households lacked even basic sanitation. But, on his tours, he recounts with sad enthusiasm all that was lost when the neighborhoods were cleared. At least 20 percent of residential buildings were owner-occupied, he notes—with small multifamily homes and lodgers making the "owner-presence" rate even higher. Jordan brings back to life lost streets such as Adams, St. Antoine, and Hastings, where there were no fewer than 350 Black-owned businesses (in Black Bottom and Paradise Valley combined). They included "the Jesse Faithful and L'il Soul Food restaurants, the Busy Bee Café, the Wolverine barbershop, the Hardin drugstore, tailoring and shoe repair shops, and the *Michigan Chronicle*," a newspaper focused on the Black community. There were famous entertainment spots, including "the Forest Club, the Horseshoe Lounge, the Music Aquarium." The blues legend John Lee Hooker specifically mentions Hastings Street and its famed Henry's Swing Club ("I think I'll go down there tonight") in his classic recording "Boogie Chillun." The heavyweight boxing champion Joe Louis and his manager had an office in the neighborhood.

And, continues Jordan, there were "mutual aid" associations—self-organized community institutions to help those in need. For elderly widows there was the Phyllis Wheatley Home of Aged Colored Ladies. The Detroit Housewives League was the "sister" organization of the Booker T. Washington Business Association; both organized boycotts of white businesses that would not hire Blacks and mounted campaigns to urge Black Bottom residents to patronize Black-owned stores, as well as helping newcomers find jobs. The thriving Detroit branch of the Urban League—established by relatively affluent Blacks to help newcomers from the rural South adjust to city life—was in Black Bottom. And, of course, churches—Catholic and Lutheran churches remaining from when the immigrant neighborhood had once been Irish, Italian, Polish, and German—and African American churches, most famously New Bethel AME, headed by the Mississippi-born Rev. C.L. Franklin, whose daughter Aretha was already in her 20s and on her way to stardom when the church was forced to relocate. Black Bottom was, in many ways, everything that latter-day pessimists about African American culture lament—filled with business entrepreneurs, small property owners, and self-help organizations.

But there had been rising concern in Detroit, observes historian Jordan, about living conditions in Black Bottom since 1943, when a fierce race riot wracked the city. It was sparked by the advent of one of the earliest public housing projects, built in response to the needs of defense workers new to Detroit. Named for the Black abolitionist Sojourner Truth, it was to be built adjacent to but not within an existing Black neighborhood.[34] And it was to be racially integrated, in no small part at the insistence of Eleanor Roosevelt.[35] A wave of cross-burnings and violence followed after the first Black families moved in. The Black residents were, after all, defense workers, not the impoverished. Jamon Jordan explains that the reaction, in addition to its evident racism, was a post-Depression hangover. Whites, he says, wanted to be sure that, upon their return from war, they would still have jobs. The fact that Blacks were being permitted to work in wartime factories, the result of a 1941 executive order by Franklin Roosevelt, and now to live in government-supported housing fueled fear and anger.

That Sojourner Truth would include Blacks as residents proved to be a spark for white mobs, which set out to attack residents and loot businesses in Black neighborhoods. "This was a true race riot," observes Jordan. "Whites were fighting only with blacks, blacks were fighting only with whites." The lesson for Detroit was not one of a need to foster racial tolerance—but, rather, that Black Bottom living conditions were unacceptable, a powder keg. Blacks were viewed as violent instigators, and Black Bottom and Paradise Valley were seen as their safe harbors, their bases of operation, threats to Detroit.

In 1946, real estate developer Eugene Greenhut first proposed their demolition—and the idea found favor with Detroit Mayor Edward Jeffries. "This area (should) be acquired by the city and completely cleared of all buildings thereon...the area then be re-planned, with the object in mind of disposing of as much as possible to private enterprise for redevelopment for housing and incidental commercial purposed after providing sufficient space for parks, playgrounds, schools and other public uses," Jeffries wrote in April 1946.[36] It was modernist planning.

The city's Common Council voted to approve the idea and to broadly condemn the neighborhood's buildings. But the idea stalled for lack of city funds to compensate property owners, many of whom were white (even when the businesses themselves were Black-owned). Indeed, Jeffries's successor as mayor, Albert Cobo, campaigned against the idea of spending city money on public housing and its attendant costs. The plan might then have stalled permanently, were it not for the entrance of the federal government and its deep pockets. The National Housing Act of 1949—which would vastly ramp up the vision of Catherine Bauer and Edith Wood nationally—included funding for "urban renewal." The few public housing projects built during the Depression and early war years would be augmented on a grand scale. As a latter-day summary by the federal Department of Housing and Urban Development would put it, the Act "Authorizes Federal advances, loans, and grants to localities to assist slum clearance and urban redevelopment."[37] At the same time, it provided funding to vastly expand public housing by up to 810,000 additional units of housing over a six-year period.

Thus would make possible both the clearance of Black Bottom and the construction of the six high-rise public housing towers known as the Frederick Douglass Apartments, to be combined with a single previously built project to become the Brewster-Douglass Homes. Doing so suited the purposes of two seemingly disparate groups: the post-war Truman Administration Democratic progressives who were convinced that public housing would provide the "safe and sanitary" conditions too many Americans lacked, and Republican Detroit Mayor Cobo, elected in 1950, whose racially charged campaign included promises to maintain white neighborhoods as white. The *Michigan Chronicle* characterized the election of Cobo as "one of the most vicious campaigns of race-baiting and playing upon the prejudices of all segments of the Detroit population."[38]

First elected in 1950, Cobo was capitalizing on response to the Supreme Court decision barring real estate racial covenants. But the idea that Detroit Blacks might be kept from moving into white neighborhoods, instead confined and concentrated in what amounted to high-rise reservations, modern and gilded before they rapidly deteriorated, would have been unlikely, if not impossible, absent the National Housing Act. Progressive housing policy did what even the race-baiting local mayor might never have been able to do for long. It was made easy, notes Jamon Jordan, because Black Bottom was such a discrete and concentrated neighborhood. "It was so easy to just wipe it out." Business owners, for the most part, received no compensation—because, notes Jordan, they owned their stores, not their property. "Public housing," observes Jordan, in understatement, "was problematic." In the short term, it provided better physical accommodations for those relocated. "A significant number of people clamored to be on the list." But "after years living there, all you would have would be rent receipts. African Americans would get the projects, whites would become homeowners. And property ownership is the way to accumulate wealth in America."

That was true not just because Black Bottom residents were drawn into the Frederick Douglass Homes, but because of the well-documented race discrimination of the Federal Housing Administration, which made post–WWII homeownership possible by insuring private mortgages. As Richard Rothstein has written:

> To solve the inability of middle-class renters to purchase single-family homes for the first time, Congress and President Roosevelt created the Federal Housing Administration in 1934. The FHA insured bank mortgages that covered 80 percent of purchase prices.... To be eligible for such insurance, the FHA insisted on doing its own appraisal of the property to make certain that the loan had a low risk of default. Because the FHA's appraisal stan-

dards included a whites-only requirement, racial segregation now became an official requirement of the federal mortgage insurance program. The FHA judged that properties would probably be too risky for insurance if they were in racially mixed neighborhoods or even in white neighborhoods near black ones that might possibly integrate in the future."[39]

In this way, too, government involvement in the private housing market can be said to have institutionalized racism. So it was that the hard bigotry of the FHA—a New Deal agency built on its fear of white reaction to Black neighbors and the racism of Southern Democrats—combined with the soft bigotry of housing reformers who believed in public housing to herd the residents of Black Bottom into a de facto high-rise reservation.

Absent public housing, much more positive counter-factuals would have been possible. As Detroit Blacks became wealthier at a time when the city's auto plants were booming, Black institutions might have renovated and otherwise improved historically Black neighborhoods. Without such deep government involvement in the mortgage market, competing banks might have sought out, rather than shut out, potential Black homebuyers. Instead, both Black Bottom and Paradise Valley would be cleared and the Douglass high-rises opened. By 2014, the six high-rise towers that had once housed 10,000 people, including the young Diana Ross of future Motown fame, had deteriorated to the point that they were demolished. Clearance had returned to Black Bottom. The nearby original site of Paradise Valley, cleared by 1956, lay fallow, notes Jamon Jordan, for years—a large empty lot where a thriving neighborhood once stood.

Ultimately, Detroit civic leaders, led by United Auto Workers president Walter Reuther, laid the groundwork for the construction of the Lafayette Park apartments—an upper-middle-class complex designed by the pioneer modernist architect Ludwig Mies van der

Rohe. The reform gaze had done its worst—clearance had been replaced by the anti-urbanism of modernist architecture in both Lafayette Park and the Douglass Homes. The thriving world of what can appropriately be called immigrant African American Detroit, judged problematic both by race-baiting local officials and federal Progressives, had been swept away by their policy tides.

CHAPTER IV

"Yes, Yes. We Weren't Dreaming": The Triumph of Levittown

The man who would do more than any other American to help realize the dream of a million homes for workers was not part of the housing reform movement. William Levitt, who would give his own name to a cluster of 17,000 homes built on former potato fields on New York's Long Island, had little or nothing in common with Catherine Bauer or Edith Elmer Wood. Levitt grew up in working class Brooklyn, the grandson of a rabbi and the product of New York City public schools. Although he attended New York University for two years, he dropped out, later explaining: "I got itchy. I wanted to make a lot of money. I wanted a big car and a lot of clothes."

Those less than idealistic goals did not preclude—and, arguably, fueled—an unprecedented boom in rapid housing construction in the years after the second World War. Levitt would disprove Wood and Bauer: The private sector could provide housing for the working man. He would become known as the

Pied Piper of an exodus from cities to suburbs—but the homes he built were far from mansions. It may seem a stretch to call this iconic new piece of suburbia a "poor side of town," especially because it was the destination for so many urban émigrés fleeing poorer city neighborhoods, but, comparatively, it was (especially as compared to latter-day suburbs). Indeed, local officials in the Town of Hempstead initially opposed Levitt's construction plans, viewing the homes as substandard. The local zoning board—itself the product of the model code and planning practices promoted by Lawrence Veiller and Edith Wood—"refused to approve Levitt's request for a waiver" that would allow for a key cost-saving design: construction on a concrete slab without a cellar. "Slab houses were rare in America at this time and the prevailing wisdom in architectural and engineering circles was that the basement was a necessity. The Hempstead Township Zoning Board denied Levitt's request for the requested change."[1] It took a campaign of public pressure orchestrated by Levitt himself, a marketer par excellence, to gain the required approval. The developer arranged for 800 WWII veterans—many crowded into city apartments with their in-laws and desperate to have their own homes—to jam the zoning variance hearing. In sharp contrast to the growth of public housing, it was individual families themselves asking for small homes they could own.

One letter submitted in favor of the proposed rent-to-own financing structure put it this way: "We have an opportunity to rent good homes on good land at a rental that is not exorbitant. Our children will be able to grow up in a decent clean community without the crowding and danger of city streets. Please remember it is important to us." Levitt himself would later recall: "The place was jammed every inch. Veterans with their wives and babies overflowed into the streets, demanding homes.

The homes they were demanding were, without doubt, a new "poor side of town" in what had been a pastoral area. Much of Long Island was known for its North Shore mansions. (The Levitt firm had concentrated on serving only that high-end market when it was first active during the Depression, building a $10.5 million "upscale residential development in Manhasset called Strathmore-on-Hudson.") The Levittown homes were not much bigger than city apartments: just 750 square feet. As the architect Witold Rybczynski would later put it, "The Levittown house had two bedrooms, one small bathroom, and an eat-in kitchen.... The porches, vestibules, entry halls and dining rooms that were standard domestic amenities in the twenties were absent from the Levittown house, which lacked even a basement. *It was bare-bones living* [emphasis added]."[2]

Crucially, this new version of the zone of emergence was based not just on offering safe and sanitary new housing, but on providing the means for ownership. This was the antithesis of the vision of Abbott and Bauer—and a return to the Helen Parrish dream of "a million small houses." Levitt would boast that, thanks to assembly line–like construction techniques, his firm could build eighteen houses in the morning and another eighteen after lunch—at a time when "most firms operating in the American real estate industry were accustomed to making thirty-six houses a year.[3]

Levitt was able to mass-market small homes thanks to a series of factors, many of which would fade slowly from American residential construction and neighborhood life. He was able to provide housing—not the poor side of town, but a poorer side—by tailoring price to the capacity of a large pool of buyers to pay. He did so, first, thanks to the zoning change granted by the Town of Hempstead. The requirement for a basement—the previous norm—would have increased cost, as would have providing a garage or a finished attic. (Both would be left to the buyer to add over time, if they chose to do so.) Nor did regulation dictate how many could occupy the homes, even though they had just two bedrooms, and some of the families were large. In another Levitt project built in suburban Philadelphia, "almost a fifth of the families had three children, and another 11 percent had four or more."[4] Doubling or tripling up was inevitable for such households, something not permitted in latter-day subsidized housing.[5] Such were the building blocks of this upwardly mobile poorer side of town.

So popular were the Levitt homes that one buyer, seeing the lot where his home would be constructed, literally lay down in joy on the concrete slab. Recalled David Glaser, "I laid right down on it. The wet slab. [My wife said], 'Get up you fool.' I said, 'Nah, look how wonderful it is.'"[6]

The heirs to the reformers understood that their dream of social housing, government built and managed, eschewing profit, had been rebuked by the commercial market and its understanding of popular preference. What can only be viewed as Levitt's triumph in housing working families was scoffed at. The left-wing San Francisco singer-songwriter and activist Malvina Reynolds, perhaps seeing the acres of Levitt-like homes sprouting in San Jose, California, derided them as "Little boxes on the hillside / Little boxes made of ticky-tacky / Little boxes on the hillside / Little boxes all the same."[7] Presumably she had not seen the apartments of Pruitt-Igoe, about which she wrote no protest song. The self-proclaimed balladeer and former Communist Party member Pete Seeger included her song in his 1960s repertoire.[8]

The homes were tailored to what buyers could afford, not affordability without regard to cost. Based on the family size tracked by sociologist Gans in his study of a similar Levitt community in New Jersey, the children would have to double up. The range of incomes meant mixes of occupations. But Levittown—and its many imitators across the country, from Skokie, Illinois, to San Jose, California—was more than just a source of inexpensive housing. Levitt self-consciously sought to build "a cozy permanent community."[9]

Levitt's father, Abraham—namesake of the Levitt & Sons firm—was not only a lawyer but a horticulturist who wrote a weekly gardening column in the *Levittown Eagle*, providing advice he hoped would be taken by the individual homeowners. (In contrast, in public housing projects all landscaping is managed by the local housing authority.) William Levitt would later recall, in what reads like a reference to high-rise, towers-in-the park life, "We made up our minds not to duplicate one basic error we found in all the other cities, namely that the individual is lost in its bigness. How we went about it was to plan some small sections of the land and give it a name like a plant, like Magnolia Hill. In this way we hope the individual will not be the occupant of a big city but rather an individual well known to his neighbors in Magnolia Hill."

A great deal follows from the fact that Levittown was a community of virtually identical homes. (There were five types offered, but the differences were minimal.) This ensured that there was a relatively limited socioeconomic range of households; those who could afford larger homes were not likely to move to Levittown, nor would those who would struggle to make the house payments. This is a powerful similarity. It was not a truly poor side of town, but it certainly was a lower-middle-class side of town in what had been a wealthier area.

The point is not that Levittown was poor, but that zoning was relaxed to permit the construction of a huge number of homes for families who were previously unable to afford to purchase a house but could now do so. The members of the zoning board who initially opposed the required variance may well have viewed the new development as undesirable because of the modesty of the houses, but they were persuaded by the emotional pitch of those packing the hearing. They were also, significantly, not asked to permit the construction of high-rise towers-in-the park public housing but, rather, single-family, if densely packed, homes not entirely out of character with their community. It is a worthwhile recipe that would, tragically, be lost.

This from the man who set out only to be rich. Levitt would almost undoubtedly be bemused by the idea that he was creating social capital—the bonds of trust that arise through community—but he was. As they had in the city neighborhoods they left behind, the Levittowners (as sociologist Gans would dub them) shared a station in life: households starting families, modest income but higher aspiration, joined by a shared fate. Not that different from the denizens of Black Bottom or Brookline's Farm.

Indeed, Levittown was forging new kinds of quintessentially American social capital. Ethnic groups that had staked out their own neighborhoods in Brooklyn—Irish, Jewish, Italian—all found themselves to be Levittowners. It can only be considered tragic that, in its 1948 legal agreement with renters or prospective buyers, Levitt & Sons required that "the tenant agrees not to permit the premises to be used or occupied by any person other than the members of Caucasian race." Levitt was convinced that the presence of Blacks—even those as well qualified as whites—would be bad for business. "I have no room in my mind or heart for racial prejudice. But I have come to know that if we sell one house to a Negro family, then 90 to 95 percent of our white customers will not buy into the community."[10] This is little short of heartbreaking in retrospect. As the historian Kenneth Jackson has put it, "There was such a demand for houses—they had people waiting on lines that even if they had said there will be some blacks living in there, white people would have moved in."[11]

Gans was alive to the missed opportunity: "Experience with residential integration in many communities, including Levittown, indicates that it can be achieved without problems when the two races are similar in socio-economic level and in the visible cultural aspects of class."[12] It's a lesson that Levitt sadly failed to apply, but also one reformers would fail to grasp. For its converse, of course, is also true: Forcing social classes together is a recipe for tension, all the more so when race is involved as well.

MY OWN POOR SIDE

There were other Levitt-like communities going up in the late 1940s and 1950s across the United States. Indeed, I grew up in just such a community in suburban Cleveland. My section of South Euclid, Ohio, was a streetscape of small wood-frame or brick postwar bungalow "starter homes"—about 1,500 of them—that went up roughly en masse, and to which lower-middle-class and working-class families moved, along with other upwardly mobile people who were spilling over the borders of then-thriving Cleveland. They were junk merchants, radio repairmen, barbers, accountants, sales reps, carpenters, contractors. No doctors or lawyers. And not many amenities as yet—a nearby main road in South Euclid was still unpaved when my family moved there in 1950.

In contrast to Levittown, this poor side of town was not ethnically diverse. It did, though, share a school district with other parts of South Euclid and Lyndhurst, populated by established WASPs and newcomer Italian and Eastern European families. The house-by-house historical records confirm what I realized in elementary school when we were asked how many would be absent on a Jewish high holiday: Virtually every household was Jewish. The names read like the wall of plaques one finds in a synagogue or the headstones at a Jewish cemetery: Jaffe, Herskovits, Goldhammer, Abramson, Greenberg.

To some extent, like the absence of Blacks in Levittown, this clustering was the product of residual housing discrimination. So-called restrictive covenants—deed restrictions that barred or implicitly discouraged sales to Jews—continued to block Jewish access to some suburban neighborhoods outside Cleveland. As Marian Morton has written in her essay "Racial and Religious Covenants in Cleveland Heights and Shaker Heights, 1925–1970," "Most covenants targeted specific racial groups...some covenants mentioned Hebrews. The covenants in Shaker Heights and Forest Hill did not mention any specific racial group but required that a property could not be resold without the consent of the developer and/or the surrounding neighbors.... The context in which these covenants were created...made it clear that the real targets, as elsewhere, were Jews and African-Americans."[13]

But, as in Levittown, this rapidly built neighborhood of small homes (two bedrooms, 1,100 square feet, unfinished attics) provided a shared sense of upward mobility. The new residents had moved up and out of neighborhoods like Cleveland's Kinsman and Glenwood, where apartments and multifamily homes were more common. And this poorer side of South Euclid would be the vehicle for building institutions—social capital.

Local Jewish newspapers of the time told the story, in ways small and big. In 1952, a Passover ad made it clear that Irving's Kosher Meat Market on St. Clair Avenue in Cleveland now offered free delivery of its "full line of poultry and choice cuts of meat" to South Euclid. Irving's would eventually move to its new customer base; my family occasionally shopped there. So it was, too, with larger institutions: "Young Israel of Cleveland has filed to permit the construction of a synagogue center on Cedar Road.... Aside from the fact that many Young Israel members reside in South Euclid...the synagogue is planned to serve the large unaffiliated Jewish population of the area, which at present does not have a synagogue."

A Jewish Community Center, relocated from the city, would be built in nearby (also heavily Jewish) Cleveland Heights, offering a settlement house–style buffet of services such as pool, gym, youth clubs, and lectures for adults. My own newly built elementary school was also involved: "Attention, Parents! A new branch of the Cleveland Hebrew Schools is being opened in the new and modern Rowland Public Schools Building on Bayard Road." Over time, the combination of housing and institutional expansion fed on itself: "South Euclid Colonial, by owner, charming 3-bedroom home, near school and synagogue," read one ad.

Notably, Jewish homebuilders—the Cleveland equivalents of Levitt—played a role, too. My home was built by the Luxenbergs, themselves the children of Polish immigrants. Mortgage deed records show that various Luxenbergs sold hundreds of homes to families with names such as Jacobs, Katz, Kleinman, Kahn, and Stein. Like Irving's Meat Market but on a far bigger scale, the Luxenbergs likely understood, because of their familiarity with the Jewish community, where demand was heading and capitalized on the opportunity. And, like Levitt, they understood what buyers like my parents could afford, and tailored—and were allowed to tailor—home dimensions to those households' budgets. They cleared land and built homes and streets abutting, though distinct from, established neighborhoods of Midwestern Protestants, as well as other new neighborhoods of similarly small homes occupied by second-generation Italians and Eastern Europeans such as Poles and Hungarians.

Social capital included, as well, a concentration of attitudes. Children were not given the expectation that they would spend their adult lives there. Memo to Jacob Riis: Poorer neighborhoods are not forever. I recall one friend's mother—the father was a television repairman—who urged the two of us to watch the television quiz show *Tic, Tac, Dough* every day when we came home from school for lunch because it was "very educational." That probably mattered less in inspiring my own intellectual curiosity than the fact that my engineer father, an outlier on the block as a college graduate, was reading Koestler and Bellow and subscribing to Max Ascoli's great magazine *The Reporter.*

But the very fact that I remember her comment shows how it reinforced the importance of education in the community. It came as no surprise that one childhood peer went on to become the Ohio Speaker of the House, another a network news executive, another a top AIPAC official, one even a major league baseball pitcher. Many more became local lawyers and owner-inheritors of family businesses. In their adult years, none would any longer live in the neighborhood.

If there was ethnic concentration, there was, nonetheless, still Americanization. My elementary school friends and I would meet the Italian kids in the seventh grade—because we shared a school district. We'd all be funneled to the same high school, the only one in the district. Some aspects of Americanization were more subtle and unusual. The neighborhood was notable for its large number of households of Holocaust survivors: the barber up the block; my friend David's father, who was a door-to-door insurance salesman (he disguised his Judaism by changing his name professionally and capitalizing on his knowledge of Hungarian); local builders; and so many others I only remember by their accents and concentration camp tattoos. Incredibly, there were families who denigrated these survivors as "damned DPs" (displaced persons), whom they apparently thought were problematic for the neighborhood. But those attitudes did not prevail. My parents looked down on such naysayers as "crude and unrefined" and remarked on how "cultured" our European neighbors were. If children were taught a lesson of tolerance, so, too, were the children of refugees, who were rapidly Americanizing: The barber's son became a basketball star. Of course, tension was minimized by the fact that these neighbors had all bought new, virtually identical small homes, demonstrating the economic wherewithal to have made it to the neighborhood.

As with the older forms of poor sides, it was implicitly understood that, countries of origin notwithstanding, everyone was there because they could afford the modest home payments—and, in key ways, shared a common identity: young families on the way up. The poorer side gave them a starting point—a home they could own, a school to which their children could walk. Like Brookline and its Town Meeting, South Euclid was its own small municipality—one in which Jews (and many decades later Blacks, who would be the successor buyers of many small homes) would become part of the local city council and board of education. Poor sides of town provided the means for those of socioeconomic and racial and ethnic difference not only to talk with each other, but to be part of a shared purpose: keeping up South Euclid.

For the adults, the move to South Euclid clearly represented an achievement. They would go so far as to announce their moves in the "social swirl" column of *The Jewish Review and Observer.* One family reported in as "Formerly of South Moreland Blvd. (Cleveland) now residing at 4049 Verona Road South Euclid." A bride whose parents lived in South Euclid announced her marriage to the son of parents who lived on E. 149th Street in the city's blue-collar Jewish Kinsman section. It was a community that was moving on up—and was proud of doing so. The city of Cleveland's population, which in 2020 stood at around 383,000, peaked in 1950 at 914,000—it was the nation's seventh-largest—and new young families were crossing the city line to achieve social mobility. Local Cleveland Jewish historian Ken Goldberg notes: "The Jewish residents of those streets [in South Euclid] mostly came from the doubles in [the city and closer-in suburbs]. They weren't used to a lot of space, and it was a very big thing for them to own single homes, with their own yards."[14]

It was not surprising that so many institutions arose to serve my corner of South Euclid. As in Black Bottom and the Farm, a shared social class and economic status among neighborhood residents can also create a sense of trust and shared purpose. Seeing housing narrowly in terms of shelter and price and obsessing about its affordability blinds reformers to that perspective. And the genie called zoning that they let out of the bottle would make construction of new poor sides of town more and more difficult.

CHAPTER V

The Unreformer and Her Lessons Not Learned

It can plausibly be said that the towers of Pruitt-Igoe first began to fall when a former Scranton, Pennsylvania, newspaper reporter without a college degree published a book about American cities in 1961. With the publication of *The Death and Life of Great American Cities*, Jane Jacobs instantly established herself as someone who might be called the great American housing "unreformer." Like Jacob Riis, she was a journalist and a newcomer to New York. A woman without a college degree became one of the most influential urban thinkers of the twentieth century. Born Jane Butzner in 1916 in Scranton, Jacobs wrote for a living, and not always for glamorous New York publications. She began her journalism career as an intern at the *Scranton Republican* and then contributed to *Iron Age*, a trade publication at which she learned the nuts and bolts of the metals industry. She learned, for instance, that non-ferrous metals were vital to modern life and how the markets for them worked. She worked briefly as a financial writer for Hearst and wrote an extended feature about Manhattan's fur district for *Vogue* and another for *Harper's Bazaar* about the crabbing culture on Maryland's Tangier Island. She was, in other words, soaking up the details of how business, culture, and the urban environment worked together when done right—the very combinations she'd go on to celebrate and whose loss she would lament—in her breakthrough masterpiece.

Jacobs always remained what her biographer Robert Kanigel trenchantly describes as "an uncredentialed woman."[1] Only gradually—and always through observation and writing—did she begin to gather the raw material for her famous criticism. Like kindred spirit George Orwell at the BBC, Jacobs became a successful propagandist for the Office of War Information during World War II. At *Amerika*, a Russian-language magazine published by the State Department during the Cold War, Jacobs was intensely edited by Marion Sanders, who would go on to *Harper's*. "The idea," Sanders would write, "is to convey some notion of the wealth and flexibility of our language." Once she'd proved herself, Jacobs wrote about the full panoply of American life—New York City high schools, American cafeterias, and, ultimately, American architecture.

As Yogi Berra is said to have put it, you can observe a lot just by watching—and Jacobs did. In Kanigel's telling, only when she took a job as a staff writer at Time-Life's glossy *Architectural Forum* did she really begin to see. Her husband, architect Robert Jacobs, had taught her how to read blueprints and she was assigned to write—positively, it was assumed—about Edwin Bacon's new urban-renewal projects in Philadelphia:

> She joined Bacon (father of the latter-day film actor, Kevin Bacon) for a tour, letting him show off all he was proudest of.... First they walked along a down-and-out street in a black neighborhood destined later for the Bacon treatment. It was crowded with people, people spilling out onto the sidewalk, sitting on stoops, running

errands, leaning out of windows. Here was Before Street. Then it was off to After Street, the beneficiary of Bacon's vision—bull-dozed, the unsavory mess of the old city swept away, a fine project replacing it, all pretty and new. *Jane,* Bacon urged her, *stand right here, look down this street, look what we've done here…*

Ed, she said, *nobody's here. Now, why is that? Where are the people? Why is no one here?*

Jacobs had, simply by looking, identified what Kanigel aptly describes as "the great gulf between how things were supposed to work in the modernist city and how they really did." The seed of Jacobs's disenchantment—nurtured by experience and observation, not theory—would blossom in ways that would eventually overshadow the world of Bacon, other architectural planners, and much of what *Architectural Forum* had featured and celebrated.

The Philadelphia trip proved to be the moment when Jane Jacobs, a forty-year-old magazine writer and mother of three, began the journey to becoming Jane Jacobs, slayer of urban-planning giants. Her public debut as a giant slayer came at a 1956 conference at the Harvard Graduate School of Design (GSD)—the very citadel of modernism. It was organized by GSD Dean and uber-modernist Josep Lluís Sert, himself a student of Le Corbusier, the godfather of "towers in the park" housing. Jacobs's appearance there was a coincidence. *Architectural Forum* editor Douglas Haskell couldn't attend, so he sent Jacobs—who'd written only one major essay on the topic—to deliver her newly formed contrarian views in his place. During what Kanigel dramatically calls "ten minutes at Harvard," she told the design profession's elite in plain English that their work led to "a social poverty beyond anything their slums ever knew."[2] The reception to Jacobs's talk was largely positive; architecture and city planning would never be the same.

Among Jacobs's fans was *The New Yorker*'s famous architecture critic Lewis Mumford. Her Harvard talk, he wrote, had "established her as a person to be reckoned with. Here was a new kind of 'expert'.... This able woman had used her eyes and, even more admirably, her heart to assay the human result of large-scale housing and she is saying, in effect, that these top lofty barracks...were not fit for human habitation."[3]

It is tempting to say that Jane Jacobs won both many individual battles (she famously led the successful effort to block a highway proposed by super-planner Robert Moses to cut through Lower Manhattan) and her war against modernist social housing. And, to be sure, her observations about the importance of a human scale in housing and neighborhoods would prove vastly influential. The title of Kanigel's biography of her, *Eyes on the Street*, captures the essence of that influence: Those watching the streets from the third floors of Boston's North End tenements or her own neighborhood in Greenwich Village helped keep neighborhoods safe. Old buildings merited preservation, moreover, not simply on aesthetic grounds but because they can be the basis for new ideas—and new urban prosperity.

But, in crucial ways, Jacobs's telling dissection of the flaws of public housing and its core assumptions would go unheeded. She was an almost poetic defender of the value of organic poor neighborhoods—places with dispersed ownership, small, locally owned businesses with their own specialties, places where urban "greenhorns"—newcomers to the city—could learn and thrive and move up and out. Such a prospect would only have been reinforced by the passage of the Civil Rights Act of 1968, which included a series of sections that would be known as the federal Fair Housing Law, prohibiting racial discrimination in the sale or rental of housing. For the first time in America, it was clearly against the law to use race as the basis to deny a home to a household that could afford it.[4]

None of these insights and celebrations were taken up by a new generation of powerful government officials who represented that they were acting in the best interests of the urban poor.

The problems of poor maintenance and crime that were turning projects such as Pruitt-Igoe into failed experiments did not deter succeeding generations of housing reformers. Indeed, the reform impulse would take even deeper root in the federal government—as reformers searched and searched for some program that would deliver on a vision of new housing that would, by its nature, provide safe, sanitary, and not overcrowded shelter and, at the same time, magically uplift the poor. Like the alchemists who sought the philosopher's stone, they would continue to try different formulas, including some that can be considered successful in narrow ways (such as the numbers of units erected) but all of which were fundamentally flawed.

By the early 1960s, the housing reform idea was deeply established in the U.S. There were more than 3,000 local public housing authorities, most of them small, managing their own sad versions of a poor side of town, neighborhoods without stores, without private owners and managed by bureaucratic overseers. Even if physical conditions were not as bad as those in Pruitt-Igoe, all embodied a series of inherent flaws. In public and subsequent versions of subsidized rental housing, no one could ever own one's own home or small building—nor aspire by proximate example to follow in the footsteps of a neighborhood's small landlords. In the name of preventing overcrowding, one was barred from taking in boarders to help pay the rent. Because rent would be fixed as a percentage of income, two-parent, two-earner households with higher incomes were tragically discouraged from forming and staying together.[5] Then there was the dull absence of neighborhood vitality. Typically, these provincial versions of Le Corbusier housing campuses had little in the way of local business. Indeed, in New York, with the country's most public housing projects, legendary public building czar Moses specifically barred stores in the projects on the dubious grounds that they might unfairly compete with enterprises outside the development—as well as a fear of some members of the housing authority board that retail uses might lead to saloons that would corrupt residents.[6]

None of this, however, was considered as a reason to turn away from government-built or -supported housing. Despite the early warning signs of dilapidation, as in St. Louis, the U.S. would double down on government-subsidized rental housing for the poor, supported through an evolving series of methods.

The "modern housing" analysis would be further empowered—supercharged, really, by civil unrest in major cities during the early 1960s—and signaled by the establishment of a cabinet-level agency, the Department of Housing and Urban Development (HUD). Although HUD had a broad mandate to improve urban life generally, there was no doubt where its chief focus lay. "The first challenge," as enunciated by President Lyndon Johnson, was "to attack the problem of rebuilding the slums." It was the era of the affluent society, when the U.S. economy was viewed as not only a powerful but perhaps even an unstoppable engine of economic growth. However, it was also seen as an engine that was leaving some groups behind. The most prominent group were African Americans, whose emigration from the rural South had peaked after World War II. That poor, formerly rural group, like urban immigrant waves before it, was living in older housing vacated by more working-class whites who were moving up and out to the expanding suburbs—to the emerging Levittowns. The racial contrast was heightened by the 1964 and 1965 summer riots in Watts and Harlem. The older urban residential neighborhoods to which Blacks were suddenly moving took on a collective national name: the inner city. Its existence was viewed as a rebuke to

American prosperity. At the same time, the headlong rush of the middle class to the expanding suburbs was dramatically diminishing the cities' populations and tax bases. A sense of national crisis emerged and was dramatically reflected in works with such breathless titles as *Cities in a Race with Time*.[7]

Had Jane Jacobs's anti-reform insights held sway, the nation would have understood that physically dilapidated neighborhoods with dispersed private ownership would improve, over time, as residents new to the cities became gradually better off. Viewing a snapshot in time as permanent is a mistake. Government, to be sure, always has an obligation to provide the core services— public safety, good schools, clean streets, convenient transit, verdant parks—that are especially important to the urban poor, just as public baths were vital to the Riis-era Lower East Side. Providing such services and accepting that the improvement of the station of the poor would be, as it had always been, a gradual process, would be in keeping with Jacobs—who, of course, also relished the building types of older city neighborhoods and what Sam Bass Warner called "streetcar suburbs." This was not a view anywhere heard as the rush to rebuild the inner city took hold. In the years to come, only one serious voice would offer such a view. In 1970, Daniel Patrick Moynihan—prescient in his understanding that there were forces at work undermining the Black family, as its marriage rates fell—urged, in a memo written in his role as cabinet-level counselor to President Richard Nixon, "benign neglect" of the race issue in America, in the belief that continued focus on it exacerbated racial division.[8] Moynihan did not address the idea of slum clearance specifically—but he was a lone voice in noting that the 1960s had seen rapid improvement in the economic status of American Blacks and that the Black community included not just the abject poor but an emergent working class—whose members, he could have added, would be alive to business opportunities in their neighborhoods, whether in property management or other ventures, just as had occurred in Black Bottom and Desoto-Carr.

Such were the ingredients for so-called slums to improve without clearance, without planning, and through the upward mobility of residents. It is a case for allowing neighborhoods to find their real level of value so as to set the stage for their long-term, sustainable renewal. All cities experience long-term real estate demand cycles. Cities can be thought of as urban ecosystems, in which various districts and residential neighborhoods, and racial and ethnic groups, fill a variety of niches and play a variety of roles. That is to say that new businesses or entrepreneurs need the inexpensive real estate and property that can be found in neighborhoods that have outlived their utility for other purposes. Vacant lots, cheap loft space, and abandoned factory buildings can become the sparks that kindle new economic ideas.

HUD's founding secretary, Robert Weaver—the nation's first Black cabinet secretary of any agency—had been clear in repudiating the idea that historically, poor side neighborhoods could simply be improved incrementally and serve as a foundation for upward mobility, as had been the case for the waves of urban immigrants who preceded African Americans to the cities.

"Our most critical domestic problem," wrote Weaver, "is improving the quality of urban life for all Americans. . . . It is our goal to *reconstruct the physical and social fabric of the American urban environment* [emphasis added]."[9] Weaver's second-in-command, Robert Wood—who came to the post after leading the Political Science Department at MIT—was just as explicit in rejecting the idea that traditional urban neighborhoods could continue to be the basis for both a good life and upward mobility. Wood told the National Association of Social Workers in 1966, "The impacted urban ghetto has, in a comparatively short period of time, become the most explosive social problem of our day."[10] This was the essence of HUD: a massive intervention in poor black neighborhoods to replace them with public housing or new variations on its theme. Thus "ghetto" housing would, per HUD, have to remain artificially inexpensive or "affordable" and would also be "decent and sanitary," in the language of the National Housing Act of 1937.

The idea that new housing was imperative—whether operated by a public housing agency, non-profit management groups, or large private managements supported by public financing and government-paid rents (all these arrangements would emerge)—reflected a bleak assumption. HUD believed that, despite America's prosperity, the poverty of what was being dubbed the Black ghetto was not transitory; the Black poor would inevitably be stuck there and should, in effect, be made comfortable in their gilded poverty.

Undersecretary Wood did acknowledge that previous groups of urban newcomers had followed what he repeatedly called the "long tenement trail to relative affluence and acceptance in American society." But he did not believe Blacks would follow in their footsteps. "The historic role of the city has deteriorated badly," he observed. "In some city neighborhoods, blight and poverty have gone hand-in-hand for generations, and the slum is no longer a way station." Moreover, he wrote, "the bus has stopped running to the suburbs and the urban poor are increasingly insulated from the larger society."

It's notable that Wood acknowledged that the slum had once been a way station. Reformers, historically, had never done so. But his acknowledgment did not deter additional rounds of policy based on the idea of the inevitability of a failed private housing market for those of modest means when HUD was established. In the wake of civil unrest, the "ghetto" would be physically overhauled with new, government-supported rental housing and massive renovation programs. The reformer's gaze continued to focus on physical conditions. A variety of new versions of housing reform emerged. Some were superficially in keeping with the insights of unreformer Jane Jacobs. The New York architect Oscar Newman gained fame and influence with the view that public housing crime was mainly due to a design problem—a lack of "defensible space" that allowed criminal activity to go undetected in high-rises. He envisioned, instead, "a model for residential environments which inhibits crime by creating the physical expression of a social fabric that defends itself."[11]

As a result, new housing projects were erected in clusters of townhouses instead of towers.[12] The expense of building and managing new public housing, combined with a new belief in "community control," led to the construction and management of low-income housing by local non-profit groups, often associated with churches. And a belief that inner-city housing re-developers could "do well by doing good" led to deep subsidies to renovate and manage existing rental properties, including a large-scale Boston project in which the local gas company invested because the building would be converted from oil to gas heat.[13]

But the HUD approach inevitably had the effect of suppressing that cycle of growth, decline, and spontaneous renewal—the poor side engaged in self-improvement and serving as a foundation for upward mobility. If poorer neighborhoods are not allowed to fall in value to their true market level, but instead are artificially sustained, the opportunities for their reuse for the gain of their residents can never be realized. Such opportunities are blocked when housing is managed as a non-profit or as a government utility (public housing) and is mandated to be permanently low-rent, or "affordable." Instead, per HUD, the ghetto was to be gilded.

Even a narrow look at the physical effects of public and subsidized housing over time is sobering. Incentives, such as low-interest mortgages, made renovating or constructing buildings more attractive than maintaining them. Thus, many HUD-financed renovations turned out to be shoddy and short-lived. The agency quickly became the owner of many buildings left behind by owners who, though they had been lured by up-front incentives, could not realize long-run profits from operating the structures as rental properties. For example, by 1978, ten years after HUD began a large-scale subsidized renovation in older inner-city Boston, it had been forced to foreclose on or assume ownership of 47 of 115 projects. As Irving Welfeld wrote, "Showcase projects had become jungles."[14] The fact that projects were privately owned should not confuse us into thinking that they were market driven. Profit-making owner-managers had simply become the subsidized agents of government.[15]

By 1983, these projects were managed and repaired by the federal government itself, as if they were public housing. In Congressional hearings, lawyers representing tenants of the Granite Properties in Boston's Roxbury neighborhood described leaky roofs, inoperable front door locks, and outright "drug supermarkets.... Tenants were provided hot water ten days out of 35."[16] It was noted, as well, that virtually all the apartments were single-parent households headed by minority women—a sad trend that has been the collateral damage inflicted by giving the poorest households priority in obtaining subsidized units and charging higher rents for two-earner households.

A similarly sad story played out in new projects modeled on the "defensible space" theory. Its showpiece was to be the Marcus Garvey Village, a 625-unit townhouse complex in Brownville, Brooklyn, built explicitly, in 1973, as an architectural contrast to the nearby towers of public housing. The village was to be akin to "college campuses. Apartment doors opened to the outside rather than onto hallways; the units had communal mews and private backyards. And yet, ultimately, the distinguishing elements delivered consequences radically different from the grand intentions."[17]

By 2013, the *New York Times* would call it a "Housing Solution Gone Awry":

> Visiting Marcus Garvey today, it is nearly impossible to imagine the excitement that surrounded its groundbreaking 40 years ago…the sense of exuberant experimentation that attended the project could not insulate it from the problems of poverty that have troubled Brownsville for decades. As one former official at the city's Department of Housing Preservation and Development told me, Marcus Garvey actually makes the ailing towers of the Housing Authority so heavily concentrated in Brownsville 'look good.' The courtyard areas, a hallmark of the design, became a nexus of the drug trade in the '80s and '90s precisely because they were shielded from public access and view. What was meant to foster an elevated sense of privacy instead contributed to criminality.
>
> Marcus Garvey turned into a home base for the Folk Nation gang. A decade ago, the complex became the target of a joint operation by the Police Department and the Federal Bureau of Investigation to combat the problem of drug- and gang-related violence in the residences. Since the construction of Marcus Garvey, the poverty rate in Brownsville has not gone down; it has gone up.[18]

All this in the name of Marcus Garvey, the Jamaican Pan-Africanist firebrand who sought to lead Blacks toward economic self-sufficiency. As with other projects named for prominent African Americans, the implicit assumption was that this would always be a predominantly Black and low-income apartment complex. Poverty was permanent.

The story in so-called "traditional" public housing had become as bad or worse. In 1989, Congress commissioned a report on the state of public housing by an entity it called the National Commission on Severely Distressed Public Housing. Over eighteen months, it visited twenty-five cities. Its final report painted a picture of physical deterioration coupled with long-term dependency, amid crime: The Commission found many things:[19]

- Residents afraid to move about in their own homes and communities because of the high incidence of crime
- High unemployment and limited opportunities for the meaningful employment of residents
- Programs designed to address distressed conditions with too little, too late
- Programs designed to assist residents of public housing that provide disincentives to self-sufficiency
- Families living in physical conditions that have deteriorated to a degree that renders the housing dangerous to the health and safety of residents
- Residents living in despair and generally needing high levels of social and support services
- Physically deteriorated buildings
- Economically and socially distressed surrounding communities

Such descriptions applied, concluded the Commission, to at least 86,000 public housing apartments—with the likelihood that, absent significant intervention, many more on the verge of severe distress would fall into such disrepair.

The inherent limits of such public housing upgrading were manifest some twenty-five years after that report was issued, in a court case involving the New York City Housing Authority (NYCHA), the nation's largest and manager of 174,000 apartments. It had once been known as "public housing that worked."[20] But in 2018, the federal government filed a complaint against the NYCHA for failure to uphold federal health and safety regulations. Federal district judge William Pauley, in a decision that led to the appointment of a federal monitor, found that "NYCHA's size is paralleled by its organizational disarray in providing any semblance of adequate housing for some of [society's] most vulnerable citizens."[21]

One might well add to this list of physical ills the fact that so many public housing tenants do not move up and out—an outcome which might help justify the projects. Instead, in New York, the average time spent in public housing is nineteen years—and 18 percent have lived in a NYCHA development for more than forty.[22] It is difficult to know these numbers with certainty— because children of public housing tenants can, in time, become the heads of households themselves. Thus, what might appear to be a new tenancy is actually an intergenerational one. I have myself met a tenant in New York's Brownsville Homes who had lived more than forty years—her entire life—in a public housing unit which she "inherited" from her mother.[23]

To the sad list of findings about public housing, one might add another indirect effect: the lack of wealth among African American households. African Americans have long lived disproportionately in public housing and later, other variations on government-subsidized housing. Of some 5 million units of subsidized housing of all types in the U.S.—including all public housing or other types that would be authorized by later generations of reformers—African Americans occupy 42 percent, more than three times their percentage of the overall population (12.3 percent).[24] Tenants, on average, occupy subsidized housing for 9.5 years. These projects, in other words, do not provide much of a springboard for upward mobility. Further data shows why. Overall, 75 percent of subsidized housing households are headed by females, while only 4 percent include two adults with children. It is thus no coincidence that Black household assets dramatically lag those of whites. A Brookings Institution study found what it called "staggering racial disparities."[25] At $171,000, the net worth of a typical white family was nearly ten times greater than that of a Black family ($17,150) in 2016."

The Brookings Institution study rightly cites the lingering effects of slavery, Jim Crow, and housing discrimination as causes of the wealth gap. Moreover, as Richard Rothstein has written, the Federal Housing Administration (FHA), which was created in 1934 to insure long-term mortgages, took race explicitly into account in rules governing who might buy where.[26] But one must also notice that, in contrast to previous waves of urban immigrants, African Americans came to the cities at a time coincident with the advent of public and subsidized housing. In ostensible benevolence, Black neighborhoods—which included Black-owned homes, businesses, and land—were cleared to make way for public housing. These are all assets that not only constitute wealth but can serve as the foundation for greater wealth. Land values change as cities change. Nominal compensation of owners at the time a neighborhood is cleared does not take into account the potential future value of such land. Businesses grow and expand; aborting them at an early stage forestalls such potential accumulation of wealth. It would be purely speculative to estimate the compound interest rate on the assets owned by Blacks in Black Bottom—but we can say with certainty that no one living in U.S. public housing, no matter for how long, owns real estate assets, by definition—in a country where home ownership is a major source of wealth accumulation. Indeed, public and subsidized housing works to undermine the value of assets held privately in the surrounding neighborhood—by luring tenants into apartments with artificially low rents. Thus lack of wealth accumulation is inherent in what is cast as assistance. Public and other forms of subsidized housing turned into a long-term dependency trap.

This is not just happenstance, but logically related to a policy that would be adopted in 1969. As maintenance problems in public housing became manifest, local authorities moved to raise rents—in keeping with the original Catherine Bauer–era idea that rental income could maintain the projects so long as profit was not involved. Tenant protests—particularly in the Pruitt-Igoe high-rise complex in St. Louis—led to a federal rule limiting rent to 25 percent of income (later 30 percent). The Brooke Amendment, named for Massachusetts Senator Edward Brooke, a Republican and the first Black senator since Reconstruction, would have profound consequences. Tying rent to income may have seemed benign—but it meant that higher income would mean higher rent. So, too, would a second household income—such as that of a spouse. In one blinkered new law, both increasing one's income and marriage were effectively discouraged. And African Americans, as a result of the dubious benevolence of reformers and Progressives to build housing projects set aside for them, would suffer disproportionately. This is not a hypothetical matter. In the strong economy during the period January 2018 to January 2019, 83,216 New York City public housing households experienced a rent increase of $112, or 22 percent on average. Their rent increased, on average, from $519 to $631 as their average income increased 16 percent ($4,271), from $26,019 to $30,290.[27]

There are deep and historic reasons for African American poverty and the gap in wealth between Blacks and whites. But one cannot ignore the fact that Blacks were disproportionately directed—or to use a housing pejorative, "steered"—to public housing. Indeed, one can infer from the fact that so many public housing projects are named for prominent African Americans that it was expected such projects would remain predominantly Black in the future, even as ownership and wealth creation were implicitly discouraged. Minority presence in public housing was not just a reflection of Black poverty, but a perpetuator of it.

One can envision a response to the severe distress in public housing that might have addressed the Black-white wealth gap: an urban Levittown, in which architects were invited to design the least expensive homes—of one to four units—to be erected on the cleared public housing sites. There would be streets and stores and entertainment—city life.

They would be privately built and privately owned, with the cost reduced thanks to the land cleared and provided. The residents of public housing would move out and up, as Levittown buyers had done. This would be not a neighborhood of poverty, but a new zone of emergence for the poor.

As fanciful as this might seem, something like it actually occurred on a large scale in the South Bronx and East Brooklyn sections of New York. And it was a dream turned reality on the part of an East Alabama former direct-mail entrepreneur, who would found an organization put on the national map by a former president of the United States. Both unfolded in what was a sort of parallel universe, even as government-subsidized and government-owned housing continued to expand and take new forms.

CHAPTER VI

The Minister and the Builder

"Ye see the evil case that we are in, how Jerusalem lieth waste, and the gates thereof are burned with fire; come and let us build up the wall of Jerusalem, that we be no more a reproach."

—Book of Nehemiah, Chapter 2, Verse 17

In Brooklyn, there might never have been more unlikely partners than a group of 34 African American churches and two retired Jewish housing developers. The Nehemiah homes project—the name is a reference to the Biblical prophet sent by the King of Persia to rebuild Jerusalem—was shepherded by a charismatic and pragmatic minister and a retired developer who turned out to have one more big project in his career.[1] These unlikely heirs to a version of the Jane Jacobs anti-reform vision were the Rev. Johnny Ray Youngblood of St. Paul Community Baptist Church and I.D. Robbins, a retired but deeply experienced private New York and New Jersey housing developer.

One can say that Rev. Youngblood was born into the idea that small homes owned by poor families should be seen as a goal, not a problem. He had been raised in New Orleans where, in the poor Lower Ninth Ward that would so often flood, most famously during Hurricane Katrina in 2006, his father built his own home. "Palmon Youngblood paid eight hundred dollars for a deep narrow patch of land on Charbonnet Street and wrought his family a house of cinderblocks and corrugated tin, pine planks scavenged from demolition sites and oak beams rescued from a ruined warehouse at work...an assembly line in an insulation factory." From that background—a neighborhood where "three-room shotgun shacks rose, filling with the refinery workers and stevedores and cleaning ladies and cooks of the black working class...the streets paved with clamshells" but where there was "perverse pride."[2] His father became a sugar refinery worker, his mother a church leader and singer on their family gospel radio program—and from those roots Youngblood would rise through historically Black Dillard University and into the ministry.

Once established in Brooklyn, Youngblood had an ambitious agenda. He sought to rebuild the Black family, riven by single parenthood, by drawing men back to the church. He saw the church as a force to reduce crime and as a potential constructive economic force in the dangerous and dilapidated part of Brooklyn where he pastored. And he came to believe in the old Helen Parrish and William Levitt idea of small homes for working people. When a community organizer for a larger group of churches known as the East Brooklyn Congregations learned of Youngblood's interest in community development, he thought of a proposal I.D. Robbins had been promoting in the *New York Daily News*, one based on small, inexpensive-to-build houses on small lots. Robbins had shopped it to elected officials for years with little success. But it found an interested audience when brought to the attention of Johnny Ray Youngblood, who would see an immediate connection between Robbins's housing plans and his own vision for a resewn community fabric.

In his account of Rev. Youngblood's time at St. Paul's and the origins of the Nehemiah project, Samuel Freedman would write: "Rev. Youngblood reacted to the evolving proposal with passion. There were so few ways in which poor people could control their own lives, least of all living in tenements owned by absentee landlords or projects presided over by distant bureaucracies. And, yet, as he often said, 'Nobody keeps a cleaner house than poor folk.' He thought of his maternal grandmother, sweeping her dirt yard every morning, or his father, building a shotgun shack with leftovers, or his mother, scrubbing it back to shine after the flood deposited mud two feet deep. What the congregants needed were homes where they could put their values and muscles to work."[3]

Youngblood forged a partnership with Robbins, an experienced private housing developer, and his cousin Lester, a New Jersey tract home builder much in the mold of William Levitt (or for that matter, Donald Trump's father, Fred, who built "more than 27,000 apartments and row houses in the neighborhoods of Coney Island, Bensonhurst, Sheepshead Bay, Flatbush, and Brighton Beach in Brooklyn and Flushing and Jamaica Estates in Queens").[4]

Youngblood and the Robbins cousins were, without doubt, unlikely partners—a charismatic black preacher and two older Jewish New Yorkers long involved in home and apartment construction. I.D. Robbins, the more public of the cousins, delighted in this incongruence, as in showing visitors (including this author) around Brownsville and the Bronx, driving his own Cadillac and pointing out "landmarks" such as the police station in the crime-ridden "Fort Apache" area. He combined a willingness to work in the poorest part of the city with a long involvement in high-level civic "good government" groups, including as president of the New York City Club. He was introduced to Youngblood as someone who "really knows how New York works." Both Rev. Youngblood and Robbins were clear in their intention to build communities that were a rebuke to public housing. As the *New York Times* would write of Lester Robbins: "The moving force behind the plan was the failure of many large postwar public-housing projects built in the inner cities for urban renewal."[5]

There were a series of foundational assumptions guiding Nehemiah—rules from the William Levitt playbook, not that of Catherine Bauer: "The homes would be owned rather than rented, so every resident had an emotional and financial stake in the experiment's success. They would be attached to one another, to hold costs below fifty thousand dollars per unit. They would be built by the thousand...to foster a renewed sense of neighborhood. And they would not rely on gifts or grants from the public sector." It was, in other words, unreformed housing.

Youngblood, the East Brooklyn Congregations, and the Robbins cousins would work to build "thousands of row houses and duplexes that revived devastated neighborhoods in East Brooklyn, the South Bronx, Baltimore and other places."[6] I.D. and Lester Robbins, like Levitt, were intent on creating affordability by reducing costs and on providing a time-tested route to upward mobility: small attached one- and two-family homes. They believed that "the simple row houses that were the original house of Eastern big cities could be constructed in New York at half the prevailing cost." They would prove their point through the use of "prefabricated components, from roof trusses to window frames to speed construction and reduce costs: Foundations for entire blocks were poured in one pass." Nehemiah would go on to build a mix of one- and two-family homes for 2,800 families in East New York (Brooklyn) and the South Bronx. Some 40 percent of the first 1,000 buyers moved to Nehemiah Homes directly from public housing.[7]

The key contrast with public housing, however, was not merely cost and design. Youngblood and the Robbinses were reinventing dispersed, private management—both by single-family homeowners and small landlords renting out lone units. They understood something fundamental: Community develops when keeping up one's property becomes part of a positive conspiracy of shared self-interest. This is so distant as to be unrelated to the institutional life of public housing.

The prospect of escaping that institutional life proved inspiring to potential buyers. Some doubled up with relatives—what housing reformers would call overcrowding or even homelessness (defined as not having one's own home)—to save up the down payment for the $39,000 homes, squarely in the Levitt tradition. Mortgage costs were just 25 percent of the income of typical buyers, who earned $20,000 a year. "The dwellings would win no architectural competitions, but they were efficient: 18 feet wide and 32 feet deep, with...front and rear yards and full basements." Pruitt-Igoe, of course, had won architectural competitions. For Nehemiah, there were modest government subsidies, including deferred property taxes and a forgivable $10,000 loan to help buyers with the required down payment. Philanthropic capital from major churches helped as well. But all this differed little, in effect, from the low down payment government-insured mortgage programs of the FHA, which had helped fuel the construction of Levittown. For Nehemiah residents, like those in forerunner zones of emergence, there were no ongoing subsidies. The homes felt like one's own and were. Improvements could increase their value. Increased home value meant increased household wealth.

I.D. Robbins—both he and his cousin were in their seventies when they embarked on Nehemiah—would tell the following to the *New York Times* when he was showing model homes in 1983:

"This is what people want. They come around here and they weep for these houses." He specifically contrasted Nehemiah with public housing, whose high-rises, he said, could never form a neighborhood. One buyer, Sandra McCollum, would say that she had despaired of ever owning a house—but once she became aware of Nehemiah through her church, she began to save money any way she could, including living with her sister for two years to reduce her expenses. In a story eerily reminiscent of early

Levittown buyers, she would recall, "There were times I said I can't. Then every day after work I'd walk over to the empty lots where they were going to build. There was garbage and abandoned cars. I tried to imagine what it would look like. I'd claim it for myself. Nehemiah was a dream and my dream was to be part of Nehemiah. When I got my keys I ran in and shouted, 'It's mine! It's mine!'"[8]

The homes were squarely in the "million small houses" tradition of Helen Parrish—a combination of modest luxuries in a small footprint. "These houses would have spacious, carpeted living rooms, tiled bathrooms, and kitchens with Formica countertops, and hardwood cabinets...but just 1,000 square feet for a two-bedroom, 1,200 in a three-bedroom. Buyers held modest jobs, including nurses, nurses' aides, hospital technicians, maintenance workers, public utility employees, letter carriers, and the garment workers. There were cooks, drivers, secretaries, manufacturing workers, and a sprinkling of white-collar professionals as well." Some 34 percent of the first group of 130 buyers moved from public housing.

By 2019, the East Brooklyn Congregations—still at work on Nehemiah expansion even after the deaths of the Robbins cousins—had completed 4,500 homes in East Brooklyn and 1,000 in the South Bronx. The church groups estimated that the increase in home values over time had "created an estimated $1 billion in wealth." The small homes idea was attracting the interest of architects who might once have been drawn to modernist projects. These include modular houses designed by SoHo architect Alexander Gorlin and assembled at the Brooklyn Navy Yard; their exteriors were infused with a palette of thirteen colors, and no two adjacent houses shared the same color scheme.

More important than such aesthetics was the wealth being built and sustained—the opposite of what public housing encouraged. The combination of a down payment requirement and advice from the churches as to whether a buyer could really afford to take on a mortgage led to there being virtually no foreclosures, even in the teeth of the 2008 financial crisis that decimated minority homebuyers across the U.S. Avoiding foreclosures helped to ensure that the values of adjoining homes would not be threatened. The *New York Times* highlighted the fact that, between the outset of Nehemiah and the foreclosure wave of 2008, only ten Nehemiah homes had gone into foreclosure.[9]

"If you could go back in the '70s and '80s and look at pictures of the neighborhood and the devastation and the flight, it's totally different," said Pat Worthy, a retired corrections officer who bought a house in the New Lots Nehemiah development in 2000. "If somebody had told you then, 'Oh, we're going to rebuild the neighborhood,' you would shake your head and say, 'No way.'" But now, she says, "You come in the summertime, everybody's grass is green, everybody's got nice flowers. People look at it, and they're totally shocked."[10]

What's more, values would rise. By the time the second phase of Nehemiah was for sale, the first phase had already doubled in value.[11] The row houses could be resold for healthy profits. Critics would say that the homes were thus no longer affordable—but for those concerned about the long-term growth of wealth among minority homebuyers such as those involved in Nehemiah, this was a triumph.

As I'd seen in the Brookline Town Meeting, a neighborhood of small owners and landlords were drawn into politics as well. That has even led, in East New York, to organized opposition to halt a new generation of higher-rise subsidized rental housing—when, in 2015, New York Mayor Bill de Blasio proposed a rezoning in the East New York neighborhood to permit the construction of three 880-unit apartment complexes. Despite a variety of neighborhood improvements as sweeteners, residents packed their local Community Board 5—part of New York's citywide system of such advisory groups—to oppose the plan. One could see Herbert Gans's warning about the friction that could arise in planners seeking to mix socioeconomic classes. One account of the controversy quoted a "Black, mixed-race homeowner" concerned that the new rental housing might "add to the number of 'Black people who are bringing down the area.'"[12] Whatever one's views of such a jaundiced perspective, it was clear that Johnny Ray Youngblood and the Robbins cousins had succeeded where so many had failed, building not just housing but a sense of community—one its members were at pains to defend.

THE GEORGIA CHRISTIAN

Far from Brooklyn, in rural Georgia, another unreformer was emerging.

As Millard Fuller would describe it, Habitat for Humanity was the culmination of a very 1960s-style cultural journey—from a comfortable life as a young entrepreneur to a search for meaning on a rural Georgia commune. It began when Fuller, a lanky, ambitious natural salesman, had established himself as a strikingly successful young lawyer and businessman in Montgomery, Alabama. While still a law student at the University of Alabama, Fuller and partner Morris Dees (an important figure in his own right who went on to found the influential left-wing Southern Poverty Law Center) had established a series of businesses catering to student needs and supplying products for local organizations to sell in fundraising drives. Fuller and Dees Enterprises continued to grow after the principals' graduation—to the point that Fuller had earned his first million by age 25.

Despite his success—with all the trappings of a big brick house, a new Lincoln Continental, a cabin at the lake, and 2,000 acres with cattle and horses—Fuller found that his marriage was foundering. He found himself returning to biblical teachings about wealth, and about relations between rich and poor, that he had learned in his youth as an active churchgoer and church youth group member. Fuller came to doubt whether wealth and a Christian life could coexist at all.

He spent the next two years as a fundraiser for Alabama's historically black Tougaloo College. Then he happened—fatefully—to visit Koinonia Farm, a rural utopian experiment near the small Georgia city of Americus. Established in 1942, Koinonia was a most untraditional place for the South; its avowedly interracial character had led to violent encounters with neighbors. With a characteristically Southern Populist religious distrust for wealth, it sought to develop a cooperative, largely self-sufficient farm for both religious, altruistic whites and Black former sharecroppers. Although the community had dwindled by the late sixties, it still cooperatively harvested fruits and pecans and sold them via mail order to a network of supporters. Perhaps it was the combination of religion and mail order that drew the Fullers. In 1968 they decided to move to Koinonia. It was there that Fuller's range of guises—from social gospel devotee to hardheaded mail-order empire builder—came together in the concept that became Habitat for Humanity.

Koinonia's charismatic founder, pacifist Clarence Jordan, planted the seed of the idea. He had a dream of building several dozen simple homes, financed by interest-free mortgages, on the Koinonia grounds for neighbors then living in shacks. With Fuller's advice, Jordan established the Fund for Humanity and raised enough money through a direct-mail campaign to build 11 houses. In September 1976, Fuller founded Habitat for Humanity—aimed at creating a much larger-scale version of what had happened at Koinonia. The organization grew slowly, building 609 houses by the end of 1983. In 1984, showing the same drive and self-confidence that had made him such an accomplished entrepreneur, Fuller drove the 8 miles from Habitat's headquarters in Americus, Georgia, to the nearby town of Plains, where he persuaded former President Jimmy Carter to lend his name and donate his time to a small, unknown regional organization. It was the turning point in Habitat's existence. Carter's participation in a most atypical Habitat event—the renovation of an apartment in the old Jacob Riis neighborhood of Manhattan's Lower East Side—ignited the public interest in the previously obscure organization that sparked its phenomenal growth. Its stock in trade would be small, single-family homes built from a catalog of types, resembling mobile homes without wheels.

In devising the program, Fuller set out some inviolable ground rules: The houses must be well built but simple; they must be owned by the families who live in them; they must be built, in part, by both volunteers and the prospective owners themselves; the "partner" families must be screened by a "family selection committee" and must pay back a mortgage over twenty years, though Habitat would not charge interest. Finally, no government funds should go toward the actual construction—although Habitat would accept government land and subsidies for infrastructure projects, and, later, use the "paid volunteers" of the national service program Americorps.

Fuller left no doubt about his unreform thinking. "The idea had been for the government to do everything," he would say. "First we gave them high-rises; then we just gave them money. They were nothing but clients, subjects. The people who devised these programs were people of good will. But they were basically saying, 'Here are a bunch of poor slobs who are barely human; let's just give them a few bedrooms and they'll be fine.'"[13]

Habitat did not hew rigidly to burdensomely high standards. It did not consider two children sharing a bedroom to constitute overcrowding, for instance. Nor was it fundamentally a charitable project, even as it expanded to urban areas. Cheryl Appline, the executive director of the Habitat chapter in poor, mostly Black north-central Philadelphia, told this author she made no apologies about the strict enforcement of mortgage payments. "We must bring people into the world of real economic life. This is no giveaway." The group encourages upward mobility too. After only three years a Habitat family may sell their home, sharing whatever profit they realize with the local chapter that helped it build. (In contrast, federally subsidized single-family homes built through the federal HOME program require fifteen years of residency before a renting family can even gain full title to the home.)

In the Helen Parrish small-home tradition, Habitat homeowners hold quite modest jobs. On a tour of Habitat houses in and around Charleston, West Virginia, I met owners who included a city garbage truck driver, a fast-food restaurant cook, a night-shift nursing home aide who also taught part-time at a Christian school, and a clerk at a convenience store. Jimmy Carter, whose administration had emphasized rent subsidies for the poor, recognized that Habitat families develop a "new sense of pride, dignity, and determination. They feel they've accomplished something on their own."

Habitat has found ways—through screening potential homebuyers as would a credit union, by finding cost-cutting methods per I.D. Robbins—to build new poor sides of towns. What Habitat does not build, however, are new, lower-income neighborhoods in better-off communities. For practical reasons, it builds mostly in poor neighborhoods. Because it needs to keep its costs as low as possible, Habitat mostly buys or receives land in areas where it's cheapest. Moreover, the organization has encountered opposition in affluent neighborhoods, fueled by the assumption that Habitat housing would be similar to public housing. "They envision a housing project, a giveaway program, problems with drugs," said Susan Sewell, a Habitat officer. Although, she added, "When they learn it's ownership, the anxiety level may go down." In that she hints at what could be a strategy for coping with the zoning barriers erected around better-off communities.

By 2019, Habitat, through a national network of locally chartered and financed chapters, had had a hand in helping 600,000 families own homes. The Nehemiah homes attracted attention and modest replicas in a handful of other cities, as well as the glowing narrative account in Samuel Freedman's best-selling book *Upon This Rock.*

To such success, one must add the rise of manufactured housing—and the "trailer parks" that consist of nominally mobile but essentially fixed-place, densely located small single-family homes. As Allen Wallis would write in 2003:

"For over three decades, the manufactured housing industry has annually produced between 20 and 30 percent of new single-family homes in the United States. Today, about 21.4 million Americans live in manufactured housing, more commonly referred to as mobile homes or trailers. The Nixon Administration was the first to recognize the essential contribution of mobile homes to the nation's housing supply, and included them in the federal government's count of annual production. Indeed, it would be hard to imagine a national housing policy that did not embrace the contribution of this housing form, which continues to supply the vast majority of affordable housing in the United States."[14] Wallis, however, noted the difficulty that zoning law posed for such homes.

"Federal acceptance runs counter to the policies of many local governments, which continue to exclude or severely limit the use of mobile homes. They justify this discrimination, at least in part, on the assumption that mobile-home land uses, especially rental parks, fail to return in taxes what their residents require in public services."

Yet notwithstanding the successes of such new approaches to building "a million small houses," they remained unappreciated. Housing reform, with its emphasis on subsidies and rentals, persisted, post Jane Jacobs, even as it assumed new and ill-considered forms.

CHAPTER VII

The Search for the Philosopher's Stone

Housing reformers—even in the wake of Pruitt-Igoe, even in the wake of the report on such widespread "severe distress"—continued to seek the philosopher's stone of some variation of public housing that would work. They embarked on a series of variations on the same themes—based on the assumption that some government intervention would and should substitute for private markets and the neighborhoods they help create—that would inevitably fail their residents. Poor neighborhoods were bad neighborhoods, they continued to assert in the Riis, Wood, and Bauer tradition. The mistakes of the public housing past could be corrected, they were sure. They would keep trying—at great expense, financially and socially.

The flaws of public housing would continue to show themselves in the new variations: its undermining of marriage and family, its physical decline over time, its threat to the building of wealth and, crucially, healthy community. What's more, the new variations on reform were costly—far more costly to build than the simple homes of the Nehemiah project. And none of these new and costly approaches considered what had been lost through generations of reform.

Following the release of the report on severe distress in public housing—at the same time Nehemiah was underway—the focus moved to saving, not abandoning, the elusive public housing dream. Steps were taken both to upgrade public housing—including, ironically, widespread demolition of projects that had deteriorated into degraded conditions—and to develop an array of new forms of low-income rental housing.

More broadly, a new reform wisdom emerged. The key problem with public housing was assumed to lie not in its fundamental ownership and management structure but in its "concentration of poverty." Instead of architectural design flaws, reformers would conclude that too many impoverished households living together were, by definition, problematic. Paul Jargowsky, director of the Center for Urban Research and Urban Education at Rutgers University, would be a leading voice of such concern. In a Century Foundation study based on census data and entitled "The Architecture of Segregation," he sounded an alarm over an increase in the number of persons, especially African Americans and Hispanics, living in neighborhoods of concentrated poverty, which he estimated to have grown, between 2000 and 2013, from 7.2 million to 13.8 million. Poor people living in such neighborhoods, wrote Jargowksy, "have to shoulder the 'double disadvantage' of having poverty-level family income while living in a neighborhood dominated by poor families and the social problems that follow.[1]

Those social problems, continues Jargowsky, disproportionately affect children. "One of the primary concerns about high-poverty neighborhoods is the potential impact on child and adolescent development. High-poverty neighborhoods produce high-poverty schools, and both the school and neighborhood contexts affect student achievement." (Note the assumptions here: Key public services such as education and public safety are cast as inevitably compromised by poverty itself.)

One might ask the question: What would it take to ensure that low-income neighborhoods could also be good neighborhoods? The next stage of the housing reform impulse would not, however, confront that question. Instead, the poor side of town was, again, judged problematic per se. A series of new variations on the housing reform impulse would follow.

The work of the Commission on Severely Distressed Public Housing led directly, most notably, to the HOPE VI program (Housing Opportunities for People Everywhere). It would include the demolition of almost 100,000 public housing apartments, including some of the most infamous projects—including high-rise towers such as the Robert Taylor Homes on the Chicago lakefront. They would be replaced with new, "mixed-income" developments in which poverty would be ameliorated according to a new theory, that it would not be concentrated. Between 1993 and 2010, the HOPE VI program demolished 98,592 public housing units and produced a total of 97,389 mixed-income units.[2] The idea of deconcentrating poverty was a basic assumption of the program, as a HUD history put it: "At the local level, developers and city governments use mixed-income housing as a strategy to deconcentrate poverty and rejuvenate neighborhoods."

As a result, there have undoubtedly been some households whose members have lived in more comfortable apartments than they could have afforded otherwise. But the key issues that have dogged public and subsidized housing—poor maintenance, discouragement of upward mobility, and regulations that discouraged two-earner households and, thus, marriage—dogged this new variation as well.

Consider the Oakwood Shores apartment complex, a $35 million Hope VI project built on the site of what was a 3,500-unit Chicago public housing complex, including the Ida B. Wells

Homes, named for the famed anti-lynching newspaper crusader.[3] Notably, the original Wells complex was built—indeed, reserved—for African Americans specifically—in retrospect another example of dubious benevolence.[4] As of 2020, its replacement, Oakwood Shores, included 524 apartments reserved for occupants with a range of income levels and managed by the Chicago Housing Authority—the same agency under whose management the Ida B. Wells Homes had become so troubled that they had to be demolished.[5] (There were plans in 2020 to increase that number to 750, for a total of 3,000 "mixed-income" units.) It would be an understatement to observe that there's good to reason to believe that the same maintenance and management problems that dogged distressed public housing would prove to be recurring. A 2020 Chicago website listing tenant reviews of apartments, ApartmentRatings, included the following comments about Oakwood Shores:

"Where do I begin? This is the worst place to ever live. My unit was broken into. This was supposed to be a secure locked unit. I did not get any assistance from management...worse customer service ever. Moved out of my unit."

"Living here has been nothing but a headache, a high turnover rate, management doesn't communicate or respond in a timely manner. Maintenance is a joke. I have about 10 outstanding work orders from a shattered back door window to a furnace that seems like it's about to explode. Peoples gas has been out 3 times for gas leaks from a faulty dryer. PESTS...omg where do I start. Roaches all in the ceilings and light fixtures and cabinets."

"Management is useless AND not friendly. Communication is nonexistent. Maintenance is EXTREMELY slow. Elevators are out months at a time and nasty. Recent blackout forced residents to have to walk up multiple flights of stairs. Elevators were out for more than 12 hours although lights came back on after 20 minutes. Broken glass in the parking lots. Garbage strewn about. In some buildings, you can smell marijuana. This is a lease violation. They do nothing. Look at the overall rating! Find another location to call home."[6]

Such are the tenant reviews of a development meant to improve on public housing. At the same time that HOPE VI was underway, another even larger federal housing initiative was enabled through tax law. The Low Income Housing Tax Credit, initiated in 1986, effectively acknowledged the management problems likely to occur in public housing authorities and looked to private developers, for-profit and non-profit, as builder-managers. The program is based on a powerful financial incentive: significant reductions (ranging from 4 to 9 cents per dollar) in federal taxes for investors. The rules are exceptionally complex, however, and the developers themselves can reap subsidies estimated as high as 91 cents on the dollar.[7]

There is little doubt that the tax credit program has led to extensive apartment construction estimated at 2 million units, located, like those of HOPE VI, in deliberately mixed-income buildings. The idea that those of similar socioeconomic status—even those of low-income—might prefer to live together in a good neighborhood was simply not considered. What's more, the overall program and the individual apartments were eye-poppingly expensive to construct; costs per apartment varied by state but ranged from $250,000 to $400,000 per apartment, in part because of the cost of the complex financing arrangements.[8] Building new apartments for those whose incomes are fundamentally not adequate to allow developers to cover maintenance costs over time—the essential physical problem with public housing itself—remains problematic. Like public housing, tax-credit buildings are attractive when the ribbon is cut—but are at risk of not being well maintained.

Warning signs of bad maintenance, along with full-blown maintenance problems, have already turned up quickly in tax-credit financed projects, notably those owned and managed by non-profit "community development corporations." By 2001, On-Site Insight, a private firm specializing in such assessments, examined 102 properties in the "affordable housing" stock and found that "seven out of 10 developments face unmet capital needs." It judged that non-profit managers such as community development corporations (CDCs) should set aside at least $2,200 more per unit per year for maintenance and repairs, and that CDCs that own older buildings, where maintenance needs loom larger, should set aside even more. CDC advocates acknowledge this problem. Francie Ferguson of the Neighborhood Reinvestment Corporation, a federal entity established to assist non-profit housing developers, observes: "The assumption is that the hard thing to do is to get housing built. In fact, the hard thing is to run it well."

The details of deferred maintenance can be chilling. An extreme case is the South Bronx group called Banana Kelly Community Improvement Association. The *New York Times* described its properties this way: "Its buildings have deteriorated; tenants have complained of no heat, of rats, of repairs not done…866 Beck Street is a building so badly deteriorated that it had to be vacated." One local Bronx community public official told the *New York Times* that "Our savior has become a slumlord."[9]

As HUD itself put the problem, understatedly, "Most property owners will confront the issue of how to meet substantial capital needs while preserving the housing as affordable."[10] Such problems are as old as the nineteenth century. One can see the outlines of this pattern as early as 1854, when the New York Association for Improving the Condition of the Poor decided to build a "model tenement" at the corner of Elizabeth and Mott Streets. Constructed by a newly formed limited-dividend corporation—

CHICAGO

Classic Chicago "two-flat" buildings. Small, multifamily buildings allow owners to earn rental income and protect tenants because of "owner presence." One of many regional architectural variations.

Credit: Courtesy of Phil Thompson/Cape Horn Illustration LLC

PHILADELPHIA

Row homes in Philadelphia. Their size and shared walls make for "naturally occurring affordable housing."

BALTIMORE

Baltimore, like Philadelphia, saw a 19th century boom in row home construction.

Credit: Photograph © iStock.com/Alexphotographic

DETROIT

Homes in Detroit's Black Bottom neighborhood. A bustling area of African American-owned businesses and residences, it was declared a slum and cleared by federally financed "urban renewal."

DETROIT

The Brewster-Douglass public housing projects in Detroit, which replaced parts of Black Bottom. Poor living conditions and lack of proper maintenance led to their demolition.

Credit: Photograph © *USA Today* Network

ST. LOUIS

The Pruitt-Igoe public housing towers of St. Louis. Hailed as a masterpiece of modernist architecture, they would quickly deteriorate and were described as a "federal slum" by a prominent sociological study.

ST. LOUIS

The implosion of the Pruitt-Igoe public housing towers in 1972,
only seventeen years after their completion. The demolition was a
turning point in the public housing movement.

ST. LOUIS

An alleyway in the Carr Square area of St. Louis, part of the city
cleared to make way for Pruitt-Igoe. As with many such so-called
slums in other cities, the neighborhood was marked by a high
degree of owner presence and local businesses.

Credit: Courtesy of the Missouri Historical Society Collections

Catherine Bauer, the influential author of *Modern Housing*, the blueprint case for American public housing. She was dubbed "Communist Catherine" by architect Frank Lloyd Wright and played a key role in drafting New Deal public housing legislation.

SOUTHBRIDGE, MA

Three-story frame home in Southbridge, Massachusetts, just one of many regional architectural styles that characterized "poor sides of town."

Credit: Photograph by Brian Vanden Brink

WORCESTER, MA

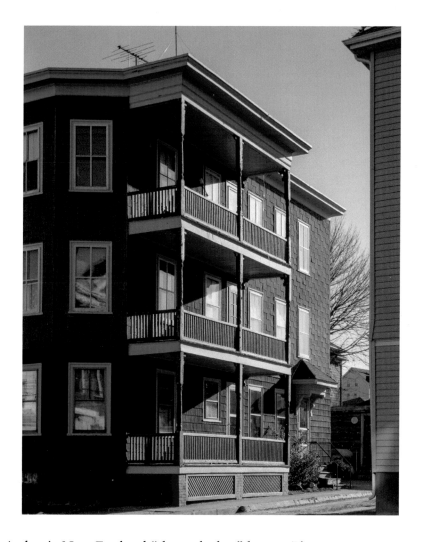

A classic New England "three-decker" house. They were described as keys to immigrant upward mobility, thanks to the rental income they provided for owners and their inexpensive construction based on shared utilities. Extended families often shared them.

Credit: Photograph by Brian Vanden Brink

Onetime newspaper police reporter Jacob Riis, a Danish immigrant, sparked interest in housing reform through his influential and celebrated photo essay, *How the Other Half Lives*, a description of conditions on New York's Lower East Side in the 1890s.

Credit: Jacob A. (Jacob August) Riis (1849–1914). Museum of the City of New York. 90.13.2.303

NEW YORK CITY

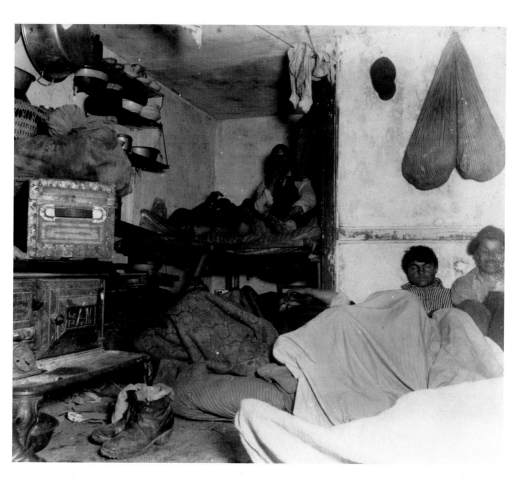

One of the many powerful photographs in Riis's *How the Other Half Lives*. Riis was a pioneer in flash photography and used photos to add power and urgency to the book.

BROOKLINE, MA

A young Ronnie Kilgallen and a local police officer in the blue-collar, Irish American "Farm" neighborhood of Brookline, Massachusetts. Like many so-called slum areas, its three-family homes provided inexpensive housing and helped build community. It was demolished through federally funded urban renewal.

Credit: Photo courtesy of Frank Moroney

BROOKLINE, MA

High-rise luxury and low-income housing replaced the Farm in Brookline.

Credit: Photograph by Howard Husock

LEVITTOWN, NY

Levittown builder William Levitt developed privately financed affordable housing on a grand scale and was hailed a *TIME* Magazine Man of the Year.

and thus meant to limit profits in the cause of providing better housing conditions than tenant incomes could support—the building degenerated just eleven years later into what would be called "one of the worst slum pockets in the city." It was sold and soon after demolished.

But the physical problems of these various forms of public and subsidized housing (the umbrella term the federal government uses), whether inevitable or unusual, are not even the worst flaws of such endeavors. Those who do manage to move into one of the limited number of low-rent units are part of not an organic community, but a social experiment based on the question of whether a mixture of household incomes will somehow make for a higher-quality environment than one of low-income households. Even to participate, one must demonstrate low income and submit to regular income checks to ensure ongoing qualification. In a system in which rent is fixed at 30 percent of income, increasing household income, just as in traditional public housing, becomes an economic burden. More income means higher rent. Marriage between two working adults leads to the same.

One must also be part of an experiment in which, thanks to the combination of high-cost construction and low-cost rent, one can appear to be a charity case. That became poignantly apparent in New York when city-subsidized mixed-income apartment buildings designated separate entrances for high- and low-income tenants; the latter dubbed their entry the "poor door."

This could not be more different—or less of a community— than Brookline's Farm, Detroit's Black Bottom, or even the wrong side of the tracks in Jim Crow Mississippi (as recalled by the Black sociologist Joyce Ladner). Those were communities in which homes and businesses were modest—and, to be sure, included, in the 1940s, privies and cold-water flats. But they were not communities in which one had to look on in envy at wealthier neighbors and wonder how one was viewed by them.

More subtly, the lower-income neighborhoods surrounding gilded tax-credit or HOPE VI projects are at risk as a result of their advent. Older homes and apartments are likely less desirable than modern apartments that rent for less than the market might demand. The pool of potential tenants for private property owners diminishes; vacancies and abandonment are a logical result. This inherently unfair government-supported housing competition logically creates a vicious cycle: Property owners in lower-income neighborhoods have less and less access to tenants, vacancies increase, and deterioration follows as rental income declines.

But the demolition—and symbolism—of Pruitt-Igoe and what it said about public housing led to another major reform direction—a push away from "brick-and-mortar" projects. In 1973, the Nixon Administration initiated Section 8 of the National Housing Act to provide tenants who would qualify by income for public housing to receive, instead, a "voucher" to use in the private housing market. Reform variations went beyond new forms of construction. What would later be called the Housing Choice Voucher program made it possible for low-income households to rent from any private property owner who would accept the voucher. As in public housing, tenant rent was fixed at 30 percent of income. The program would come to house twice as many households as so-called physical public housing, but it would bring with it many of the same problems, along with some new ones.

Vouchers appealed not only to liberal housing reformers—always concerned about housing "affordability"—but also to conservatives, who saw it as a less expensive alternative to public housing. That support overlooked a great deal. Receiving what amounted to a coupon that could only be used for one thing—rent—inevitably distorted personal decisions in a series of subtle ways, as people sought to obtain or retain a financial benefit.

Living with another breadwinner—whether a spouse or just a roommate—became a handicap that led to higher rent. Indeed, one had an incentive to keep one's own income down in order to avoid higher rent (or lose other government benefits, such as food assistance or low-cost medical insurance). It should not be surprising that voucher tenants stayed an average of almost ten years in the program, even in an era (starting in 1996) when cash public assistance—"welfare"—was capped at five years.

Nor did the voucher program lead with any certainty to a reduction in the feared concentration of poverty. A combination of tenant preference and the willingness of property owners to accept voucher tenants resulted in what Baltimore congresswoman Barbara Mikulski called "horizontal" rather than high-rise "ghettoes." Scholarly research supported her view. A University of Cincinnati study found exactly such concentrations, which it termed "hot spots."[11] Nor was Cincinnati an anomaly. A subsequent study looked at cities nationwide and concluded that "Examining the 50 most populous U.S. metropolitan areas...households using vouchers are more economically and racially segregated than an extremely low-income comparison group."[12]

Nor would geographic dispersion of voucher households ensure a happy outcome. In a devastating essay in *The Atlantic* on the impact of replacing public housing with housing vouchers, journalist Hanna Rosin reported that, rather than being reduced as poverty was less concentrated in housing projects, crime had metastasized. She reported on the work of University of Louisville criminologist Geetha Suresh in tracking local patterns of violent crime. "She had begun her work years before, going blind into the research: she had just arrived from India, had never heard of a housing project, had no idea which were the bad parts of town, and was clueless about the finer points of American racial sensitivities. In her research, Suresh noticed a recurring pattern, one that emerged first in the late 1990s, then again around

2002. A particularly violent neighborhood would suddenly go cold, and crime would heat up in several new neighborhoods. In each case, Suresh has now confirmed, the first hot spots were the neighborhoods around huge housing projects, and the later ones were places where people had moved when the projects were torn down. From that, she drew the obvious conclusion: "Crime is going along with them."[13] Rosin reported on how that change looked close-up in one such city, Memphis, where middle-class Black homeowners found themselves to be the targets of gangs who had migrated from the projects.

I observed the same phenomenon in my own journalism focused on the predominantly Black south suburbs of Chicago, to which voucher tenants relocated as public housing projects in that city were being leveled. The trend upset Black businesspeople and homeowners who had made their own way up and out of lower-income neighborhoods in the city—following what Robert Wood had dismissed as the no-longer extant "tenement trail."

In south suburban Chicago, which has one of the highest concentrations of voucher holders in the country, middle-class African American residents complain that they thought they'd left the ghetto behind—only to find that the federal government was subsidizing it to follow them. Vikkey Perez of Richton Park, Illinois, owner of Nubian Beauty Supply, expressed her fears that the small signs of disorder that have come with voucher tenants—the unmown lawns and shopping carts left in the street—could undermine the neighborhood. "Their lifestyle," she says, "doesn't blend with our suburban lifestyle." Kevin Moore, a hospital administrator and homeowner in nearby Hazelcrest, complained that children in voucher homes go unsupervised. Boom boxes play late at night. "I felt like I was back on the West Side," he says, referring to the Chicago ghetto where he grew up. "You have to remember how to act tough."[14]

Such flash points would continue to emerge. In 2019, a Washington, DC, program to use rental vouchers to move low-income households into a middle-class apartment complex in the affluent Cleveland Park area set off sparks. Wrote the *Washington Post*: "Some tenants with vouchers say they have been made to feel unwelcome by their new neighbors, a dynamic that has unavoidable undertones of race and class in a largely white neighborhood."[15] Middle-class tenants, for their part, complained of social problems, including drug and alcohol abuse, on the part of formerly homeless tenants relocated to their building.

These reports, it must be noted, have been challenged by social scientists, notably by a research team at the Furman Center at New York University. In an analysis of crime data from ten cities, its study found "no evidence that an increase in households using vouchers resulted in increased crime in a neighborhood.... Our results show that community resistance to households with vouchers based on fears about crime is unwarranted."[16] But the study did find that "households with vouchers tend to settle in areas where crime is already high." A similar finding was reported by a UCLA study.[17] Furman notes ongoing popular concern about the crime-voucher link. This disjunction between expert and popular opinion may suggest either a race or a class bias. At the same time, it may suggest a concentration of social ills and building maintenance issues in specific buildings with a concentration of voucher holders—and that relatively small hot spots may not shift the larger community crime rate significantly upward. Consider these social media comments posted about an apartment complex with a concentration of voucher holders in Warrensville Heights, Ohio, where Biden Administration HUD Secretary Marcia Fudge once served as Mayor:[18]

"Stayed in these apartments for a year and it had to be the worst year of my life...apartment was/is infested with bed bugs and they knew about it. The management does nothing to help with anything. Other tenants are really noisy which you can clearly hear through the thin walls."

Another posted comment: "This should be called Warrensville Townhouse Projects."

Sheer relocation from a dysfunctional low-income neighborhood to a "better" neighborhood will not lead inevitably to better lives for those relocated. It is, rather, the opposite: the process of making positive life choices—with regard to employment, education, and marriage—that makes upward mobility possible. That process is helped immeasurably if one can start in a poor side of town where one holds assets, even modest ones, and in which municipal services like public safety, public schools, and public recreation are well provided. *A healthy poor side of town is the launching pad toward a zone of emergence.* The voucher program, like its reform predecessors, short-circuits that healthy process. Indeed, not even good housing is guaranteed. If voucher holders find themselves living in substandard conditions, they have a difficult challenge in pressuring for improvements: The government is paying most of their rent, typically through direct deposit to a property owner's bank account. They lack the leverage that tenants normally enjoy.

Strange as it may sound, the voucher program, by requiring that the income transferred to a voucher holder be devoted exclusively to the cost of housing, denies what might be called the right to overcrowding; that is, the right to make one's own decisions about how to spend one's income and what sacrifices to make in order to achieve long-term goals. Should one decide to "double up" with a relative in order to save money for a home down payment—as happened with the Nehemiah buyers—the voucher terms would discourage that.

There is evidence that new, low-income immigrants are willing to make that tradeoff. For instance, in New York, the city with by far the largest public housing and housing voucher system in the U.S., 11.1 percent of households in poverty are Asian, but only 4.7 percent of public housing occupants are. Asians, along with non–Puerto Rican Hispanics such as Dominican immigrants, are also those who most commonly live in overcrowded conditions in the city—23 and 26 percent, respectively. In contrast, Blacks account for 25.8 percent of the city's households in poverty but occupy 42 percent of the city's public housing units and only 14 percent of overcrowded units. This underscores, again, the counterproductive benefit that African Americans, as earlier arrivals to the city than other urban immigrant groups, "enjoyed" because they occupied and remained in public housing, where the rules effectively barred the family savings that short-term doubling up can realize.[19]

In keeping with their historic pattern, however, housing reformers would not give up on the voucher program—and would remain convinced that a way could be found to ensure that it would be the key to socioeconomic upward mobility.

At the same time, even if healthy, low-income neighborhoods had been understood to be better than the schemes of housing reformers, following the "tenement trail" to a brighter future would have remained difficult. New versions of the "zones of emergence" were increasingly difficult to build, thanks to the long-term impact of an earlier aspect of housing reform: municipal zoning. Its regulations and their impact not only would diminish the variety of housing and locations available to the aspiring, but also would inhibit the formation of a local politics that included a socioeconomic mixture. Put another way, forces were aligned against the growth of new versions of the Brookline Town Meeting, in which janitors had an equal voice with lawyers.

CHAPTER VIII

The Legacy of Lawrence Veiller: Zoning Out Zones of Emergence

The history of the spread of U.S. zoning—those local rules that dictate what sorts of housing and commercial structures may be built and where—has no moment equivalent to Jacob Riis's publication of *How the Other Half Lives*. Indeed, Dartmouth College economist and historian of zoning William Fischel makes the case that some sort of local zoning was inevitable, as property owners sought to keep homes and factories, for instance, in separate parts of the city.[1] "Zoning has for a century enabled cities to chart their own course. It is a useful and popular institution, enabling homeowners to protect their main investment and provide safe neighborhoods."

But there is a key figure in the history of the spread and specifics of zoning and whose efforts foreshadowed ill effects of zoning that has become extreme, in inhibiting even new versions of Levittown, let alone the Farm or Black Bottom. He was Lawrence Veiller, the director of an organization he helped found in 1910: the National Housing Association. Veiller, like Catherine Bauer and Edith Wood, was born into an affluent family. He was the son of an Elizabeth, New Jersey, stockbroker. His work with the New York poor through the Charity Organization Society—which, like its counterparts elsewhere, sought to provide a central clearinghouse through which the poor could seek assistance—led him to Jacob Riis and concern about New York's tenement conditions. Moving beyond the exposé, however, Veiller became a leader of, first, the Tenement House Committee, a citizen group, and in 1901, the New York State Tenement House Commission. Its Model Tenement House Law aimed not at prohibiting multifamily buildings but at ensuring adequate light, fire exits, and running water.

Veiller's enthusiasm for laws regulating what sorts of housing might be built would not be confined to New York City—nor would his influence. In 1910, he co-founded the National Housing Association and would become editor and key writer of its magazine, *Housing Betterment (A Quarterly Journal of Housing Advance)*. As the historian Roy Lubove would put it, "after 1910, Veiller was constantly on the move, visiting various cities at the request of people who had prepared housing laws and wished to submit them to the acid test of his consideration."[2]

But Veiller also had his own Model Housing Law that he hoped cities would adopt, a law that dealt with much more than tenements and their housing codes. With it, Veiller became the Johnny Appleseed of zoning. By 1920, he had graduated from his success in influencing states to adopt building codes regarding tenements, and was pushing for localities to adopt zoning laws—specifically, his Model Zoning Enabling Act.[3] As a template, Veiller was a key architect of a suggested standard state zoning enabling law, developed by the U.S. Department of Commerce in 1922 when future president Herbert Hoover served as its secretary.[4] But because zoning must be locally adopted, the federal guidance and even state laws did not mean that Veiller's mission had been accomplished. Thus was Veiller "on the move" in his advocacy. *Housing Betterment* reported on—and cheered—municipalities across the country that were adopting zoning laws for the first time, codes that included districts reserved for single-family homes set back on relatively large lots. "Portland, Oregon has adopted a comprehensive Building Zone Ordinance which, it is believed, will do much to foster industry, stimulate home ownership and comfortable home conditions for industrial workers, as well as to make the city a more orderly and convenient place to live."[5]

Veiller and the Association were by no means agnostic about what sorts of new homes should be permitted. In his Model Housing Law, the proposal he traveled the country to promote to municipalities, Veiller provided a wealth of details about the extent of space, lavatories, and more. But, in comparison to the sort of regulation that would build upon it, especially in the 1960s and after, Veiller's early proposal for zoning law was far from draconian. Residential homeowners, per Veiller, would have to agree, block by block, to petition a municipality to zone a neighborhood as residential. Even then, one side of a street could continue to have commercial uses—stores, not stables (unless local owners agreed to such). It was assumed that two-family homes would be interspersed with single-family dwellings, providing the means for buyers who needed rental income to afford to become homeowners.[6]

This is not to say that *Housing Betterment* was particularly sympathetic to the housing needs of upwardly mobile immigrants. Its publications, recall, notably included "The Menace of the Three-Decker," whose author, Prescott Hall, attacked the New England three-family house, one of the most successful forms of working class "zone of emergence" housing in America, as little more than a firetrap. (Indeed, "zone of emergence" authors Woods and Kennedy had singled out the three-decker for special praise: "One cellar, one water and gas main, one plumbing shaft for three families, divide the cost of these by three for each family. The number of tenants that can be accommodated is, of course, multiplied by three."[7])

But even the relatively modest restrictions of the early zoning advocates set the stage for regulations that were so much more extreme that they can well be considered qualitatively, not just quantitatively, different. Zoning, especially as it affected the opportunity for housing to serve as rungs on a ladder of upward mobility, would go far beyond the unobjectionable idea of separating industrial and residential districts or even apartment and owner-occupied blocks.

Crucially, zoning, as it has affected residential development, has come to be virtually synonymous with single-family zoning. Looking back on almost a century of the effects of residential zoning in the U.S., Robert Ellickson of Yale Law School described a "zoning strait-jacket: the freezing of American neighborhoods of single-family homes."[8] Ellickson makes two key points. Single-family residential zoning dominated land-use regulation in America's suburbs, where population growth and prosperity grew throughout the twentieth and early twenty-first centuries. His analysis of 37 suburbs in California, Connecticut, and Texas found that "municipalities had set aside 91% of their residentially zoned land exclusively for detached houses. For many local officials, only a detached house seems to satisfy the American Dream of homeownership. A townhouse or condo does not suffice."

Such zoning, by its nature, is a barrier to the development of lower-cost, lower-income sides of town—that is, zones of emergence. What's more, notes Ellickson, it acts not only as a straitjacket limiting what sorts of housing may be built (he takes the phrase from an early judicial decision that blocked the advent of zoning), but "freezes" uses in place, precluding the increase of the amount and variety of demand in the housing market.

(Of course, the same can and should be said of public housing, which typically remains in place even as neighborhoods change around it, blocking the advent of new uses that might benefit poor and affluent alike.)[9]

"Local zoning politics," writes Ellickson, "almost never allows a landowner to replace a house with a denser residential use, such as a duplex, set of townhouses, or apartment building."[10] He notes that a "Massachusetts agency found that more than 99.7% of the state's land in single-family use in 1970 remained in single-family use in 1999, almost thirty years later." Ironically, the "freezing" of American neighborhoods even extended to Long Island's Levittown, which could not have been built in the first place had William Levitt not packed a public hearing in order to obtain a zoning change permitting homes without basements to be built. Ellickson notes that when legal covenants limiting the neighborhood to single-family uses expired in 1975, "Levittown NY residents successfully lobbied the Town of Hempstead to permanently freeze the single-family character of all Levitt subdivisions."[11]

The U.S. Census Bureau has noticed the trend in its examination of all U.S. housing construction, not just that in suburban residential areas: "In the 1970s and 1980s, there was a trend toward building more multifamily homes (about three in ten to one-third of all homes built in those years), which began to decline in the 1990s (17% of all homes built in those years) and has held steady at that rate in the 2000s."[12]

Put another way, neighborhoods such as Brookline's Farm or Detroit's Black Bottom—even if each housing unit had its own bathroom, plenty of light, and other amenities—could not be built in most of America in the post-zoning era. Their relative density—though far less than that of, say, the Lower East Side in the Riis era—was simply not permitted. Lost were the opportunities for the upwardly mobile poor to afford homes and accumulate wealth thanks to the rents of on-site tenants; lost was the assurance to tenants that on-site owners would be likely to maintain the premises; lost was the possibility for small business owners to live above their shops; lost was the chance for the renting poor to be inspired by the example of the property owners from whom they leased. Lost was the sheer social fabric of a neighborhood in which residents, like those of the Farm or Black Bottom, shared community institutions such as schools and churches and understood themselves to be part of a common American story of shared interests, maintaining their neighborhood through their own efforts rather than having to rely on the benevolence of a "program."

The predominance of single-family housing to the exclusion of other types, even owner-occupied multifamily dwellings, along with the "freezing" that Ellickson describes, has been accompanied by another powerful trend inhibiting new lower-income, lower-cost zones of emergence: not just single-family zoning but large-lot zoning, requiring one or two or more acres of land per house. Levittown houses, like those of Nehemiah, are closely clustered compared to what has followed. In a landmark 1968 essay, David Schoenbrod was the first to describe the trend. In his essay "Large Lot Zoning Note," he wrote:

"Twenty years ago the typical new metropolitan dwelling was an apartment or a house built on a small lot. Even in prestigious suburbs, the well-to-do often placed their expensive homes on lots much smaller than one half acre. Today, on most undeveloped land around large cities, minimum lot-size zoning prohibits all development save single-family dwellings on lots that are very large by traditional standards. Even by 1960, of the vacant land zoned for residential use within fifty miles of Times Square, eighty per cent was off limits to apartments or houses on lots of less than one half acre. More than half was zoned for single-family dwellings on lots of not less than one acre, and minimum required lot sizes ranged up to five acres.

"For a metropolis as large as New York, large lot zoning has meant that several million fewer people can live in the suburbs closer to the city."[13]

The language of the comprehensive plan of Little Compton, Rhode Island—an affluent seaside community within commuting distance of Providence or Boston—is representative: "There is one residential zoning district in the Town, referred to as Residence (R) District. The creation of new lots within the residential zoning district requires a minimum of two acres."[14]

Not even new versions of Levittown would be likely to pass through such exclusionary gates. Not surprisingly, as large-lot zoning became the norm, homes themselves became larger. The move to larger lot requirements has led to the construction of larger and thus more expensive homes. The Census Bureau noted the trend in 2011:

"The size of the average home built today (in the 2000s) is considerably larger than those built in earlier decades. The median square footage of a single-family home built in the 1960s or earlier stands at 1,500 square feet today. In comparison, the median square footage of single-family homes built between 2005 and 2009 and between 2000 and 2004 stand today at 2,200 square feet and 2,100 square feet, respectively."[15] By 2019, that median had risen further, to 2,301 square feet.[16] Nor do such figures capture the trend toward far larger homes, upward of 5,000 square feet, colloquially known as McMansions—a term of some aesthetic derision that has long since replaced "little boxes." The combination of Ellickson and Schoenbrod has had the effect of pulling up what can be called the housing ladder of opportunity.[17]

Put another way, the housing trends described above are about much more than housing. They inevitably inhibit economic upward mobility. They limit the socioeconomic range—yes, the "diversity"—of a great many municipalities, where the higher costs of larger homes limit such residential variety. They even limit the political influence of those who find they cannot afford

HOW THE RIGHT ZONING
CAN SAVE A NEIGHBORHOOD

The Boston neighborhood called Mt. Bowdoin was known in the 1980s as one of the city's most dangerous and dilapidated when Gerard Hurley and Iris Dupont bought the house at 7 Bowdoin Avenue. It was a house with a long history dating to 1868, when a New England Yankee carpenter named William Hunt bought the vacant lot atop the hill and built what would grow over time to an 18-room home. It's trite to call a big frame house rambling, but this one does indeed ramble across the lot on the hill named for the colonial patriot James Bowdoin, also the namesake of Bowdoin College. The house was erected, and expanded in increments, in what amounted to a nearly rural area of what was the independent New England town of Dorchester before it was absorbed into the city of Boston and became a patchwork of ethnic neighborhoods.

If the walls of 7 Bowdoin could talk they would tell a quintessentially American story through the lives of its residents. In the century-plus before Hurley and Dupont bought the home for $150,000 in 1986, it had been home to Yankee school teachers, Swedish immigrants who had added rooms and begun renting to boarders, and an unmarried hippie couple taken with the adventure of moving into what had become a predominantly Black neighborhood by the 1970s. Hurley and Dupont, African Americans who'd grown up in the public housing projects of what had become a dangerous Dorchester, saw the area's problems as a backdoor advantage: They could buy a large, lovely home inexpensively.

The key to its affordability was, however, #7's three rental apartments, added during the Depression by Swedish immigrant owner Harry Kleberg. "Without the rental income," recalls Dupont, "we could never have paid the mortgage." Crucially, this was no illegal or informal conversion. When they bought it the home was, per city regulations, officially a four-unit structure: the owners' section and three small rental units. The effect, however, was not just to let Hurley, a onetime airport skycap, and Dupont, a designer and visual artist, buy a home which, by 2020, was valued at nearly a million dollars. Its non-frozen non-single-family zoning helped bring to Mt. Bowdoin a woman, Dupont, who would prove to be a one-person, Jane Jacobs–style neighborhood protector.

As a newcomer, Dupont joined the Mt. Bowdoin Improvement Association, a decades-old neighborhood group. When the elderly previous president moved away, "Everyone in the meeting said Iris should take over," she recalls. "I was elected." In the pandemic summer of 2020, Dupont opened the carriage house she'd converted to an art studio to neighborhood residents for a "We Paint" day. She confronted—calling in ranking police officials to help—the drunk, loud, and rowdy crowd that had taken over the lovely Mt. Bowdoin Green on the hilltop. And she was working to find ways to pressure the out-of-state property owner of a six-family building that was filled with housing voucher tenants. (She and Hurley had had their own problems with a voucher tenant, to whom they rented as a response to a request for help from a non-profit housing assistance agency. "They trashed the place," as she puts it.) Not only was the six-family building not being well kept, but those were the same residents turning the park into a threat to the working people of Mt. Bowdoin getting a good night's sleep.

But broadly, Iris Dupont was convinced Mt. Bowdoin was on the way up. A once-abandoned commuter rail station nearby had been reopened. The trip to downtown Boston traversed just four stops now, instead of a long bus ride to a subway. She sheepishly observed, positive, that "We're even seeing Caucasians moving in." That, of course, is another way of saying that a larger pool of potential buyers is considering the neighborhood—which is how neighborhoods avoid abandonment and, instead, revive, saving lovely old homes like 7 Mt. Bowdoin.

None of that happens automatically, however. Improvement occurs thanks to the Iris Duponts of the world—who choose not to be passive when problems arise. Yet she would never have lived on Mt. Bowdoin in the first place, had what was originally a single-family home been stuck in that state, frozen. Instead, it was a step up from public housing for her and her husband—and the daughter they raised there. They were able to accumulate financial assets—even send their daughter to private school—not because they'd been relocated to a higher-income ZIP code, but by doing what it takes to increase the value of their home by being part of the Mt. Bowdoin Improvement Association. The lesson is this: Communities that are convinced that by clinging to zoning that may inhibit newcomers from buying homes they are preserving property values may actually be compromising them.

to move to suburban areas, where the size of municipalities, compared to big cities, is far smaller. In a local government in a municipality of 50,000 and a city council of nine members, for example, one's vote is more impactful than in a city of 500,000 with a nine-member council. As I've written with Wendell Cox, "Consider the comparative figures for the City of Columbus, Ohio, and Bexley, a municipality surrounded by Columbus. Columbus has seven city council members for a population of 860,000—a ratio of one council member for 123,000 residents. Bexley also has seven city council members but for a population of 13,700—a ratio of one council member for 2,000 residents. New York City, with 8,540,000 residents, has 52 city council members—large by the standards of such bodies—or one council member for 164,230 residents. In contrast, the suburban village (municipality) of Malverne, Long Island, has four members of its board of trustees for a population of just 8,500. That is one legislator for each 2,100 residents. Los Angeles, with 3,976,000 residents, has only 15 council members, one representative for every 265,000 residents. More people are represented by each Los Angeles city council member than live in Buffalo and more than 19,400 US municipalities."[18] The contrast with my old town of Brookline—which I'm admittedly casting as something of an ideal case, notwithstanding its urban renewal sins—59,000 residents are represented by no fewer than 240 Town Meeting members—one member for just 245 residents, and one for just each 162 registered voters. It's a place where it truly feels that every vote counts—and indeed, as I've already noted, the author was once elected to his Town Meeting seat by a single vote.[19]

It is inevitable that a range of housing types and costs within a given municipality will lead to a spectrum of socioeconomic groups being politically represented, with pressure for their specific needs being part of the political debate. The wealthy may prefer private schools for their children, but lower- and middle-income voters will push for public school funding. The wealthy may be members of private golf and beach clubs, but other groups will push for public parks and recreation.

The trends toward large-lot, single-family, "frozen" zoning combine to underlie what has come to be called "exclusionary zoning," aspects of which have been noted since David Schoenbrod's 1968 essay. The 1991 Advisory Commission on Regulatory Barriers to Affordable Housing, formed by then Housing and Urban Development Secretary Jack Kemp, observed that "the negative impact of overregulation has caused concern in the affordable housing debate for several decades. In the past twenty-four years, no fewer than ten federally sponsored commissions, studies, or task forces have examined the problem, including the President's Commission on Housing in 1981–1982. These study groups have made many thoughtful recommendations, usually to little avail. In the decade since 1981, the regulatory environment has, if anything, become a greater deterrent to affordable housing: Regulatory barriers have become clearly more complex, and apparently more prevalent."[20]

To that emphasis on the sheer cost of housing has been added the concern that the upwardly mobile—even those who are well educated and come from backgrounds of significant economic advantage—cannot afford the housing costs in America's most prosperous regions, as a result of regulation driving up cost and limiting supply. As zoning scholar Fischel of Dartmouth has put it: "It appears that the rise of land use regulation in the 1970s has reduced migration from low-income regions of the United States to higher-income regions. This seems to have contributed to the rise in income inequality in the last 40 years."[21]

Yet the gates of restriction stand. That they do involves the financial advantages enjoyed by the current owners and the aesthetic choices of local planners. It may well reflect race and class bias, as well. But a crucial and far less appreciated reason for continued barriers has been the ill-chosen tactics of those who have sought change. Present-day housing reformers, like their predecessors, have, by misunderstanding the dynamics of housing markets and the concerns of citizens, created far more controversy and backlash than they have helped those of modest means. The ghost of public housing haunts their efforts. Changes in zoning—really, making changes in the character of American residential communities—will not occur by hectoring or attacking those who are in the position to make such change.

CHAPTER IX

Maximum Feasible Opposition: The Lesson of Mario Cuomo

In 1972, a then-obscure Queens lawyer named Mario Matthew Cuomo received a call from the mayor of New York, John Lindsay. The mayor was turning to Cuomo for a mission that other, more prominent city figures had already declined, thanks to its controversy and apparent thanklessness. At issue was an 840-unit, so-called "scattered site" federally subsidized low-income housing apartment complex. The city had decided to build it in the Queens neighborhood of Forest Hills, a solidly working- and middle-class district, whose side streets off Queens Boulevard were lined with wood or brick one-to-three-family homes, mainly occupied by their owners. The idea of a low-income rental "project" in the neighborhood had set off a firestorm of community opposition. As the prominent New York journalist Murray Kempton put it: "Low-income translates as black, young and poor, and Forest Hills, if it boasts few remnants of fashion except the West Side Tennis Club, is white and middle class."[1]

The famously liberal Lindsay Administration's approval of the project had already set off a political backlash by the time Cuomo was called in to put out the fire somehow. Members of the Forest Hills Residents Association had already dogged Lindsay's abortive presidential campaign in Florida, where the Jewish voter mattered greatly. The Association's leader, one Jerry Birbach, threatened to "publicly place his house for sale to a black and would lead to a massive emigration from Forest Hills."[2] In effect, it was Cuomo's task to convince those in a neighborhood he knew well, and where he was known for previous legal work for citizens' groups, to calm down about the whole thing. "Delegations of the enlightened" hoped he would convince project opponents to dial down their anger.

But a funny thing happened as Cuomo came to understand the situation and recount it in his thoughtful and revealing memoir, *Forest Hills Diary*. He realized—or likely knew beforehand—that opponents had a point. He imagined taking project supporters to one of New York's existing public housing projects. "I shudder to think of the reaction they would have to Queensbridge and some of the other projects I've seen." Cuomo understood that there was very little profit in treating the opponents of the project as simple bigots; it seemed to him that local people could be both "sincere and reasonable" when they argued that "any substantial influx of the poor and the Black carries the danger of crime and decay." Cuomo imagined their vision of "the husbandless, black welfare mother with three children, living in a hovel in the midst of a ghetto that is pure filth."

Cuomo, what's more, was stunned when, on his own initiative, he sought out groups of middle-class Black families in another section of Queens to sound them out on how they would view such a housing project.

"I went to Cunningham Park early this morning knowing that a lot of the blacks from South Jamaica (a section of Queens, not the Caribbean island) would be there in family groups. These blacks were fortunate enough to have homes of their own in Hollis, Queens. They unhesitatingly said that they would not want the project in their neighborhood."[3]

Ultimately, Cuomo forged a compromise: The size of the Forest Hills project would be reduced by half. But in historical terms, that is not the important part. Forest Hills demonstrated that policies aimed at locating subsidized rental housing for those significantly poorer than those in the surrounding communities was a route to community opposition.

One might think that some adjustment in tactics could have been adopted by those concerned about such important goals as the upward mobility of minorities and the racial integration of neighborhoods (or at least the rights of African Americans to live wherever they chose). That has not proven to be the case, however. Instead, the push for similar approaches elsewhere continued, in the process guaranteeing opposition by overlooking some of the most basic truths about American neighborhood patterns.

Indeed, government-led deconcentration or dispersion of the urban poor would be at odds with an unwritten yet powerful norm. Residential patterns are largely shaped by socioeconomic status and residents' sense of accomplishment, resulting in an urban spatial structure with varied housing styles and types, linked to social class, in different neighborhoods.

This powerful but informal system has long been recognized by scholars, starting with the Chicago School of Sociology in the 1920s. Geographer Philip Rees observed that "Socioeconomic status is a universal sorting principal in American cities."[4] He found that education, income, and occupation strongly correlated with residence. Similarly, Michael White has noted that residence and social status are interrelated: "Time and again it has been argued that socioeconomic status is the principal differentiator in the metropolis. Poor neighborhoods with residents who work in lower-status occupations and have lower levels of education are found to be separated from the high-status neighborhoods in the urban mosaic. Educational attainment and occupation are good overall indicators of a neighborhood's status. The level of income, correlated with these two characteristics, is the most direct indicator of a household's ability to 'purchase' status, or at least purchase a residence in what is regarded as a high-status neighborhood."[5]

Herbert Gans's observations, based on his work in Levittown, have remained true. Forcing residents with different socioeconomic statuses to live in the same neighborhood is a recipe for tension. As Gans writes, "If one group is threatened by another's demands, intolerance may…increase."[6] Engineering people to live together raises the question of whether new, subsidized residents deserve to be in a community that houses those who moved there based on what they understood as decisions based on self-improvement, self-sacrifice, and upward mobility, not ongoing monthly government subsidies.

Such observations have stood the test of time, as evidenced in 2004 by economists Anna Hardman and Yannis Ioannides. "For the vast majority of US households, neighbors' incomes and other characteristics are the market-driven outcome of individual choices. Households' tastes for housing space, quality and access to jobs and amenities, together with their incomes and assets, define demand for housing types and locations. Prices set in the housing market determine what housing units and neighborhoods households can afford."[7]

In the 1960s, during a time when race-based discrimination was common, Gans observed that rival ethnic groups such as the Irish, Italians, Jews, and Poles (some of whom were not even considered white by nineteenth-century nativists) made common cause in Levittown. Most Levittowners understood that there was a virtuous conspiracy of self-sacrifice, shared

values, and smart personal decisions in terms of work, education, marriage, and thrift, resulting in desirable communities
characterized by high-quality public amenities, such as a low
crime rate, high-quality public schools and parks, and clean
streets, among others.

The lessons of Forest Hills have continued to play out. A 1969
Massachusetts law, for instance, was designed to allow builders
to bypass local zoning limitations on density if "at least 20-25%
of the units have long-term affordability restrictions."[8] Because
another Massachusetts law pressures localities to set aside 10
percent of all housing as "affordable," the law has some teeth.
"Chapter 40B," named for the section of state law it amends,
was, notably, passed in the wake of a state law aimed at forcing
local school districts with racially diverse student populations
to integrate individual schools. Urban politicians, who felt that
suburbs were in effect insulated from the controversial law, promoted Chapter 40B—first to force suburbs to carry some of the
burden for helping minorities advance, and later simply to help
"open up the suburbs" to lower-cost housing.[9] There is no doubt
that its impact has been fairly substantial. By 2011, it had "been
used to produce over 60,000 units in almost 1,200 developments
(built or under construction), including over 42,000 rental units
and about 18,000 ownership units." The housing is not, it's worth
noting, set aside for those of the lowest income, with just "over
half (over 32,500 units)... reserved for households with incomes
below 80% of the area median."[10] It's also the case that the population of the state grew by more than a million between 1970 and
2018, from 5.7 to 6.8 million, and housing prices rose dramatically during the same period. Chapter 40B had, in that context,
a modest impact on housing production. Moreover, because it
insists on "permanent affordability," it limits the returns even
on those 18,000 units whose construction it spurred, which are
not rentals but owner-occupied units.

But apart from such limitations, the most notable ongoing effect of Chapter 40B has been undying controversy. Time after time, 40B projects, even if they include households other than those of the lowest income, are viewed in much the same way that residents of Forest Hills viewed low-income housing, as recorded by Mario Cuomo. As one newspaper account summarized matters in 2019, 50 years after the law was passed:

> Want to ruffle some feathers? Bring up the subject of 40B in Massachusetts.
>
> The affordable-housing program, known technically as Chapter 40B, has existed for five decades and is the subject of endless debate across the Bay State.
>
> The subject, however, is often clouded with confusion surrounding the program, how it exists and why it creates so much friction in a state where affordable housing is so tough to find.
>
> …a stigma hangs over affordable housing because of its association with low-income housing. In many cases, neighbors fear affordable-housing developments will transform a neighborhood and drive down housing prices.[11]

Put another way, the ghost of public housing continues to haunt any policy that sets explicit income limits on new apartments. That newspaper account was accompanied by a photograph of a large crowd of protestors packing a zoning hearing in the town of Easton, Massachusetts, many carrying placards with 40B circled and crossed out and reading, "Save Williams Street." 40B, continues the account, "has become something of a bogeyman."[12]

A 2009 federal court decision affecting suburban Westchester County, New York, provides another telling example.[13] The decision used the leverage of federal financial assistance to the county and what the court viewed as an inadequate fair housing law enforcement plan to force the county to appropriate $50 million of its own funds to help build 750 units of subsidized housing, including 630 units in some of its wealthiest enclaves, where less than 3 percent of the population was black and less than 7 percent Hispanic—and to market them especially to those groups. A suburban area of nearly 1 million residents north of New York City, Westchester is a mix of very affluent suburbs (such as Scarsdale) and cities with a spectrum of income groups (Yonkers, White Plains, New Rochelle). Local officials, although forced to settle the suit, were irate; indeed, a new county executive (the top local office) was elected in the same year as the court ruling, in part because of his opposition to what the *New York Times* called "a controversial fair housing plan."[14] "There's no evidence of exclusionary zoning based on race," he would assert.[15] There is good evidence he was right.

Westchester County, in fact, boasts a significant Black and Hispanic population. Westchester's 131,000 Blacks represent 14.2 percent of its total population, and its 144,000 Hispanics make up 15.6 percent—both mirroring almost exactly the population of the nation as a whole. The crux of the lawsuit: Westchester's minority population is not evenly distributed throughout the county, but concentrated in the county's cities to the south, including Yonkers, New Rochelle, and White Plains. As it once did for Italians and Jews, this area serves as a stopping point on the path of upward mobility for families leaving behind the Bronx section of New York City, on the county's southern border.

That northern Westchester has so few minority families compared with the county's south is a sign of unlawful segregation, the accusers said. In key testimony in the court case, Queens College sociologist Andrew Beveridge claimed that "income level has very little impact on the degree of residential racial segregation experienced by African-Americans," leading to what he called increased "racial isolation." Put another way: Minority-group members were not living in the places where their incomes would predict they should be living. They were said to be living in ghettos, even though they could afford better; thus, segregation existed in Westchester and, by extension, in any affluent place where minority households are few.

There are at least two problems with this line of reasoning. First, even in the super-wealthy parts of Westchester, Blacks are only slightly underrepresented, based on what their incomes would predict. As of the 2000 census, Scarsdale was 1.5 percent Black; Pound Ridge, 1.2 percent; Harrison, 1.4 percent. The numbers may sound low, but there simply aren't many very affluent Blacks in the entire county. Only 2 percent of Black households in Westchester earned more than $200,000 in 2000—a total of 911 families—compared with 12.6 percent of white households. Small wonder that there weren't many Blacks in the county's richest locales. Race discrimination was not required for that to be the case.

Probably more important, however, is that if the Beveridge claim were true, you'd expect Westchester to be full of higher-income Blacks who, prevented from moving into the more affluent areas that their incomes would predict, were stuck living near lower-income whites. But census data showed that this isn't the case. Blacks in Westchester generally have *lower* incomes than their white neighbors do. According to the 2000 census, for instance, Blacks in New Rochelle had a median family income of $55,000; whites, $72,000. In Tarrytown, the figures were $50,000 and $82,000; in Hartsdale, $79,000 and $100,000. In Westchester as a whole, Black household income in 2000 stood at 51 percent of that of whites, and Hispanic income at 44 percent. Though lower Black household incomes aren't anything to celebrate, the data does not indicate that those who can afford to move into high-cost areas face discrimination. This should be a national goal: ensuring that anyone who can afford to buy or rent is not denied on the basis of race.

In that context, however, a good argument could be made that fair housing based on income had actually been achieved in Westchester, even as it was being made a poster community for exclusionary practices. But fair housing was not really the goal of the suit, which was supported by the Obama Administration's Department of Housing and Urban Development, which viewed the mere existence of higher-income communities with low percentages of minorities as problematic. As Ronald Sims, HUD deputy secretary, said in regard to the court decision, wealthier communities are obliged to offer "choice" to those of lower income so that the poor, too, can "enjoy what I call the fruits and benefits of an established neighborhood."

But Sims had the process of upward mobility exactly backward. Improving one's lot in life is not a function of rubbing shoulders with the better off. Rather, and again, it reflects myriad good decisions and successful struggles: staying in school, learning a skill, and getting and staying married, to name a few. Better-off towns and districts—including not just the wealthy of the working class and lower middle class—are not demonstrations of privilege and unfair advantage; they are hard-won achievements, reflecting the larger contributions of their residents.

Indeed, such views were expressed by African American Westchester residents in response to the federal court housing order. Just as misgivings about the Forest Hills project had included the Black families wisely sought out by Mario Cuomo, the *New York Times* reported the following:

> "As an African American who happily resides in one of the aforementioned targeted for this deplorable lower income housing, I am appalled at this decision to reward those individuals who…chose the easy way out instead of dedicating oneself to hard work….My wife and I worked hard to be able to purchase a home and PAY TAXES in one of these towns, just like everyone else who resides in them."

Another reader made a similar point:

"As an African American, I am tired of the practice of placing government housing in otherwise middle-class and affluent neighborhoods....All it does is reinforce a stereotype that all African Americans are laggards when it comes to educating ourselves, rising socially and advancing economically. It is not as though there aren't African Americans already living in these neighborhoods in Westchester."[16]

But even more important than the unfortunate social class friction precipitated by the ideas guiding the Westchester order was the ongoing belief that it represented that poor neighborhoods could not, by definition, be good neighborhoods—launching pads for upward mobility, not dead ends. Opportunity would be said to be available only in so-called "high-opportunity" ZIP codes.

That idea would guide a policy infatuation with a variation on the Westchester approach that latter-day reformers dreamed of implementing widely. Superficially it was similar to the idea of bringing the social classes together in a shared municipality, but the terms are entirely different. The idea of "Moving to Opportunity" stemmed from an experimental randomized federal housing mobility demonstration program, conducted between 1994 and 2004 in five cities: Baltimore, Boston, Chicago, Los Angeles, and New York.[17]

A 2016 analysis of its impact by the prominent economist Raj Chetty attracted wide attention for its apparently positive findings. His analysis focused on the life prospects of children raised in low-income families that participated in the MTO program, and found that children who moved to lower-poverty neighborhoods before the age of 13 have higher college attendance rates and earnings and lower single-parenthood rates. As Chetty put it: "The findings imply that offering families with young children living in high-poverty housing projects vouchers to move to lower-poverty neighborhoods may reduce the intergenerational persistence of poverty and ultimately generate positive returns for taxpayers."[18] As Chetty put it, further: "Low-income children are most likely to succeed in counties that have less concentrated poverty, less income inequality, better schools, a larger share of two-parent families, and lower crime rates."[19] Chetty's findings set off interest in increasing the value of housing vouchers such that low-income households could move to "high-opportunity ZIP codes," where rents were higher—and for local laws requiring property owners to accept such voucher holders. (Such laws are known as bans on "source of income" discrimination.) For example, Julian Castro, when he served as Secretary of the U.S. Department of Housing and Urban Development in the Obama Administration, said, "We're interested in, in terms of the Housing Choice Voucher program, how do we enhance mobility to get families who choose to live in higher opportunity areas into those higher opportunity areas?"[20] Similarly, social scientists Barbara Sard and Douglas Rice focused on reforming the housing voucher program, encouraging voucher holders to locate to low-poverty areas.[21] Furthermore, Daniel Hertz went so far as to advocate that housing vouchers—i.e., individual household rent subsidies—should be made an entitlement.[22]

There is a compelling narrative implied: an intervention to rescue families with children from housing projects and move them to places with better schools, parks, and public safety. But there are a number of reasons to be cautious about this latest version of housing reform. Not all the social science analysis of Moving to Opportunity is as positive. Previous work had been sanguine in its assessment when looking at the effects other than those for young children, finding "no significant overall effects on adult employment, earnings or public assistance receipt."[23] Two years later, a Harvard research team "did not find evidence of improvements in reading scores, math scores, behavior or social problems, or school engagement, overall for any age group."[24]

Certainly, Chetty's later work provides additional and positive findings. But it is important to note that positive effects were limited to those families who moved when their children were young, and were less positive the older children were at the time of the move. This matters much in terms of any federal housing program, whether it is one that uses higher-value vouchers (those providing higher rent subsidies) to allow the poor to pay the higher rents of more affluent communities (and perhaps require landlords to accept them) or one that would use financing tools, such as the federal Low-Income Housing Tax Credit (LIHTC) subsidies, to support the construction of subsidized housing in non-poor communities where land costs are higher and subsidies would therefore produce fewer units. Indeed, in practice, participation in federal housing programs is based not on motivation or demonstrated benefit for select groups, but on eligibility based on income level, among other factors. It is difficult to imagine—even as a legal matter—limiting participation to those households whose children are pre-adolescents, those for whom the newer research by Chetty specifically finds a benefit. The matter of scale is important, as well: Will a government intervention be able to scatter all those considered "disadvantaged" among higher-income municipalities and neighborhoods? The greater the scale, the greater the cost to taxpayers—and the greater the likelihood of the sort of resistance first encountered by Mario Cuomo in Forest Hills. Indeed, in 2020, the Trump Administration criticized and repealed the Obama-era regulation known as Affirmatively Furthering Fair Housing (AFFH), which extended the Westchester approach to communities across the

U.S. that received federal "community development" funds from HUD. President Trump trumpeted the rollback in a way that demonstrated he well understood the link homeowners made between federally supported low-income housing and the unease experienced by residents of Forest Hills in Mario Cuomo's day. In two public statements on Twitter on July 29, 2020, the president put it this way: "I am happy to inform all of the people living their Suburban Lifestyle Dream that you will no longer be bothered or financially hurt by having low income housing built in your neighborhood. Your housing prices will go up based on the market, and crime will go down. I have rescinded the Obama-Biden AFFH Rule. Enjoy!"[25]

Such comments were written off as racism. Former HUD Secretary Julian Castro said, "It's a naked ploy to drum up racial fears and white resentment."[26] But it's important to consider the subtle messages delivered by such an intervention as they relate not to suburban homeowners, but to the ostensible beneficiaries of such programs. The program's very name says a great deal: One must move in order to have opportunity. The idea that low-income neighborhoods could also be good neighborhoods—where the streets are safe and the schools effective—is implicitly discounted. What's more, in contrast to Brookline's Farm or Point, those "moved to opportunity" have arrived at their new location on terms quite distinct from those of their new neighbors. They are not the owners of small homes, or landlords renting to a family in that home. They have arrived as part of a social science experiment—there to benefit from the benevolence of those who have built and sustained the community. They are, to be blunt, the beneficiaries, not the contributors. They have entered through a "poor door" and cannot help but understand their situation differently than those who have saved for a down payment, built a two-earner family, and entered through the poor side, not the poor door.

Moreover, there is a deep reformer's assumption here: that it is self-evident which neighborhoods are better. One student of the question of why some voucher holders tend not to choose to "move to opportunity," Ingrid Ellen of New York University, observes, "Social ties also likely play a role in potentially limiting the neighborhoods considered by voucher households. If people choose to locate near family and friends, and disadvantaged individuals tend to have disadvantaged social networks located in higher-poverty neighborhoods, then this may restrict where voucher families looks for housing."[27] This, of course, makes the non-mover decision appear unwise—but it might just as well be characterized as a choice between a community with which one has much in common and another in which one would be an outlier. Like Herbert Gans's West Enders, some households value things that middle-class reformers do not.

Desirable communities are neither inevitable nor inherited. Rather, they must be built and maintained day by day, meeting by meeting, one swept sidewalk at a time. This virtuous conspiracy, however, is predicated on a sense of commonality. Programs such as Moving to Opportunity cannot help but put that sense at risk. As the Harvard political scientist Robert Putnam found, "[N]ew evidence from the US suggests that in ethnically diverse neighborhoods residents of all races tend to 'hunker down.' Trust (even of one's own race) is lower, altruism and community cooperation rare, friends fewer." Putnam expresses the hope of overcoming "such fragmentation by creating new, crosscutting forms of social solidarity and more encompassing identities."[28] That is a hope of this book. Doing so, however, will mean finding ways of persuading, not mandating, those who have erected walls around their communities to lower them. Might it be desirable for wealthier jurisdictions to have lower-cost sections, in which true neighborhoods based on common backgrounds and concerted personal effort could form? Yes—and that's a theme of this book. Indeed, and ironically, much of Westchester County, like so many older so-called "streetcar suburbs," is dotted with them.

But "opening the suburbs" will not be widely achieved through confrontational court orders or complex housing policies aimed at engineering a "deconcentration" of the poor based on the assumption that such an approach will inevitably improve life prospects. Yet the latter, especially, is the most recent version of the housing reform impulse.

CHAPTER X

Slums of Hope

E ven as the U.S. has struggled with the interrelated questions of housing policy and upward mobility, the historic driving force behind public housing and its subsequent variations has not gone away. For the developing world—from South Africa to Brazil, India to Kenya—the term "slum" is applied to districts far larger and more populous than New York's Lower East Side or London's East End ever were. Indeed, the United Nations has said that "more than 880 million people are estimated to be living in slums today (2015) compared to 792 million in 2000 and 689 million in 1990."[1, 2]

The question thus presents itself: Will they, or should they, be the rationale for new generations of reform-inspired "social" or government-subsidized housing? Put another way, what can be learned from the unhappy history of American housing reform policies that can be preventively applied elsewhere? In practice—not only in developing countries but even in surprisingly similar settlement areas in the U.S.—the old modernist housing reform ideas are losing out as pragmatic steps to simply improve daily life in these new, vast poor sides of the world are taken.

As *Planet of Slums* author Mike Davis writes of these vast informal settlements, "the cities of the future, rather than being made out of glass and steel envisioned by earlier generations of modernists, are instead being constructed out of crude brick, straw, recycled plastic, cement blocks and scrap wood."[3]

The harrowing descriptions of the conditions in Third World slums in a tide of twenty-first-century books on the subject, including Davis's, are in the Riis tradition. The novelist Wallace Stegner described this journalistic impulse pointedly in his short story about a photographer assigned to document slum conditions. "Dutifully, Prescott went on with his job, documenting poverty for humanitarianism's sake and humanizing it as best he could for the sake of art."[4]

But many of the book's overall assessments and reform prescriptions are decidedly not in the Riis tradition. A relative consensus has formed about how best to address the new slums' problems, and, surprisingly, it appreciates what the UN calls the "positive" elements of slum life, shaped by a population characterized not as oppressed and helpless but as resourceful and creative. Journalist Robert Neuwirth, for instance, extols slums as places where "squatters mix more concrete than any developer. They lay more brick than any government. They have created a huge hidden economy.... [They] are the largest builders of housing in the world—and they are creating the cities of tomorrow."[5] In keeping with this encouraging trend, the UN even describes the Third World's informal settlements as "slums of hope." Slums are being understood differently—an understanding that leads down a different housing and development path.

What, exactly, are slums? Some, especially in the developed world, are once-affluent neighborhoods gone to ruin; others were newly built public housing. But most are gigantic, tightly packed concentrations of flimsy shacks and shanties that rural migrants have built on the outskirts of cities—what the UN calls "vast informal settlements that are quickly becoming the visual expression of urban poverty."

Most of these settlements are in the developing world. Of the 924 million slum dwellers worldwide in 2001, 554 million lived in Asia, in such cities as Mumbai and Kolkata in India and Karachi in Pakistan. Another 187 million lived in Africa, in places like Cairo, Durban, Johannesburg, and Nairobi. And 128 million lived in Latin America and the Caribbean (famously, in the favelas of Rio de Janeiro and São Paulo). Only 54 million were in developed countries.

The UN blames the massive migrations from rural areas either on population growth that the countryside cannot sustain or on economic prescriptions said to emphasize commercial agriculture over small farming, thus driving the poor off the land. Whatever the cause, this "urbanization of poverty" has resulted in the large-scale erection of primitive forms of shelter, either on public land or on private land owned by absentee landlords. Water, sanitation, and other utilities are usually lacking, making the incredible overcrowding even harder to bear.

One doesn't forget visits to such places. When, during the late apartheid era, I traveled through Black townships outside the beautiful seaside city of Port Elizabeth, South Africa, I met families living in what reportedly were converted Boer War–era British-built huts with dirt floors. Water poured only from a communal tap, and there was no electricity. UN official Naison Mutizwa-Mangiza recalled for me his first trip to Nairobi's Kibera, Africa's largest slum and home to 700,000: "There is the poor physical quality of the environment, overcrowding, houses so close together, tin-roofed, walls often of mud, with just a very small window. But it is the smell from lack of sanitation that hits you in the face. You have to jump over numerous small trickling drains, filthy and filled with smelly water mixed with other types of waste, including feces. There are no toilets; people use plastic bags in the night for defecation and then throw these out in surrounding dumps and streams." [6]Riis's Manhattan, even at its roughest, was never that squalid. True, some 20,000 residents' shacks once squatted on the site of what became Central Park. And certainly the Lower East Side was terribly crowded. But even the worst Orchard Street tenements were actual buildings, not tin-roofed shanties with dirt floors—some, in South Africa, left over from British military installations built during the Boer War.

To put contemporary slums in perspective, it's important to review what Riis got so wrong—and how his views set policy in a counterproductive direction. For Riis, the slum's biggest problem wasn't population density, lack of sunlight, or even disease. It was what it did to the character of its residents. Slums were "nurseries of pauperism and crime that fill our jails and police courts; that throw off a scum of forty thousand human wrecks to the island asylums and workhouses year by year; that turned out in the last eight years around half a million beggars to prey upon our charities...because, above all, they touch the family life with deadly moral contagion." The "contagion," Riis warned, included a lack of "domestic privacy"—meaning the potential exposure of children to adult sexuality. "His entire book," write Bonnie Yochelson and Daniel Czitrom in *Rediscovering Jacob Riis*, "could be read as a plea for understanding how the tenement environment itself deformed character." The slum dweller's grim surroundings kept him from developing bourgeois virtues.

This "environmental determinism," as housing historian Alexander von Hoffman calls it, led reformers to try to improve the behavior and prospects of the poor by replacing the slum environment altogether. A better living environment, it was felt, would produce better people. Riis himself promoted the "model tenement": privately built apartments for the poor, constructed to higher standards made possible by investors' willingness to forgo normal profits. No wonder Riis has wound up cast in the company of heroic reformers of the Gilded Age and early Progressive Era, such as Upton Sinclair and Ida Tarbell. In his new biography, Tom Buk-Swienty gushes: "Riis forced Americans to confront the squalor of immigrant conditions, and he demanded that those immigrants not be treated as second- or third-class citizens."[7]

But this uncritical view ignores how Riis's environmental determinism led, gradually but inexorably, to the advent of large-scale public housing, which would have destructive unintended consequences.

All such bestowed benefits risk discouraging beneficiaries from behaving constructively—saving money and accumulating assets, say, or making the prudent life choices, such as marriage and education, that truly help households "move up" to better neighborhoods. In other words, improved housing is an effect, not a cause, of the bourgeois virtues that Riis held dear.

That so many Americans could rise from the slums into the middle class shows, moreover, that the Lower East Side was filled with such virtues. The neighborhood was a beehive of effort, including that of immigrant entrepreneurs who built and ran apartment buildings. In Riis's book, writes Czitrom, "the complex day-to-day negotiations and textured lives of tenement dwellers simply disappear into a riot of pathology."[8] Yochelson and Czitrom quote historian Jared Day, who described "the tenants who scraped together small sums to buy leases; they were the grocers, butchers, boarding house keepers and barbers who pooled their resources...and they were the immigrant bankers...who took the savings of average ethnic workers and invested them in local housing." In Riis's view, "the tendency of the tenements and of their tenants is all the time, and rapidly, downward," as he wrote in *How the Other Half Lives*. But in a dynamic economy, it turned out, he had things exactly wrong. As New York's Tenement House Museum now refers to its historic building, tellingly, not as slum housing but as an "urban log cabin," slums, made as livable as possible through public investment, can be a starting point for upward mobility, a portal through which impoverished rural people pass as they become urbanized.

This is also how we should think of the sprawling new slums of the developing world: not as doomed, deforming environments but as the low-cost housing built for (and by) displaced, formerly rural people drawn into the modern urbanized economy and energetically aspiring to a better life.

In Hong Kong—hardly impoverished but a powerful magnet for China's rural poor, especially after the 1949 Chinese Communist Revolution—I was once taken to the top of one of the city's ubiquitous four-story apartment buildings. There I found one of Hong Kong's 50,000-plus "unauthorized building works": three tiny boxes housing families that stole electricity from the floors below. In the event of a stairwell fire, they could escape this high-rise shantytown only by jumping off the roof. But aspiration was abundantly evident, too: I saw school uniforms neatly laid out on tiny mattresses and a kitchen table with a hot plate. In the South African township that I visited, similarly, one saw plenty of shacks but also larger, self-built homes with their own Honda electric generators.

The Economist captured this atmosphere of activity and hope in a December 2007 article about Dharavi, a Mumbai slum. Dharavi had "maybe a million residents crammed into a square mile of low-rise wood, concrete and rusted iron," yes, but its residents were also "thriving in hardship." Small "hutment" factories, for instance, exported leather belts directly to Wal-Mart. Dharavi, the magazine observed, was "organic and miraculously harmonious...intensely human."[9] The FinMark Trust, a South African housing think tank, has found no fewer than 335,000 businesses in one Johannesburg slum, one in seven home-based.

They include everything from hairdressers and bars to welders and furniture makers.

These informal sprawls, for all their problems, may well prove to be a source of new products—and refinements and improvements of existing products—helping to fire future economic growth. Jane Jacobs envisioned this transformative churning in her landmark book *The Economy of Cities*—a process in which the poor, making the best of their circumstances, create substitutes for expensive imports and eventually develop superior products for export. Having exposed the folly of modernist architecture, Jacobs went further, pushing back against Engels and his views on "foul air" and asserting that slums could be hotbeds of innovation.

"Early in this (20th) century, it was conventionally assumed by American philanthropists that poverty is caused by disease. Healthy people, it was reasoned, would be more productive, have more initiative, be more capable of helping themselves, than people in ill health.... Measures to combat disease turned out to be quite successful at combating disease, irrelevant for combating poverty.... To seek 'causes' of poverty...is to enter an intellectual dead end because poverty has no causes. Only prosperity has causes.

"It can be overcome only...in the development work that goes on in impractical cities where one kind of work leads inefficiently to another...the little movements at the hubs that turn the great wheels of economic life."[10]

Happily, the debate about slums is no longer dominated by the project of replacing or eradicating them and sweeping away all those little movements and personal initiatives. In fact, that approach has become politically incorrect. "There is no drive to replicate the bureaucratic welfare-state housing-policy approaches of the mid-twentieth century," observes Columbia University's Elliott Sclar, a lead author of the UN's 2005 *Improving the Lives of*

Slum Dwellers.[11] Even the Harvard Graduate School of Design—once led by followers of the architect Le Corbusier, the father of high-rise public housing—has sponsored an approving exhibit on the "nonformal cities of the Americas."

Policy has shifted toward improving slum conditions incrementally, helping residents gradually become better off, even if still living within the slums. South Africa's Reconstruction and Development Programme, for instance, has subsidized over 1 million modest, 344-square-foot single-family structures that families own and, over time, are expected to improve. This is Nehemiah in the Third World. The World Bank, too, whose work in developing countries long emphasized grand infrastructure projects like dams and bridges, is now financing modest but significant improvements in the world's informal settlements. In Brazil's informal favelas, it helped some 900,000 people obtain "potable water piped directly into their homes," and about 1 million receive sewer services. Cost: just $84 per capita. Similarly, the bank has invested $192 million in the Mumbai slums to build privately managed pay toilets, used by more than 400,000 people. The UN's Top Ten list of "slum upgrading actions" ranks "installing or improving basic infrastructure" first and makes no reference to government-subsidized replacement housing.

The incremental approach mitigates the risk of the kind of dependency that welfare states have unwittingly fostered in the poor in the past. After all, cities provide regular neighborhoods with sewage and water systems, too, so giving slums such services doesn't give their residents an incentive to stay put. Further, incrementalism doesn't undermine slum dwellers' sense of personal agency. Living in a shanty that you can call your own and improve over time is preferable to moving into government-owned housing.

Those who see potential, not hopeless degradation, in the world's new slums do disagree on something important. Does slum dwellers' upward mobility depend on their actually owning their houses? Or will they eventually prosper if they're simply granted the formal right to stay—but not to sell?

The second option is known as "security of tenure." "It doesn't matter whether you give people title deeds or secure tenure," writes proponent Robert Neuwirth in *Shadow Cities: A Billion Squatters, a New Urban World.* "People simply need to know they won't be evicted." As Sclar observes, "secure tenure" would make it easier for slum dwellers to join the formal labor force, knowing that they aren't at risk of arbitrarily being forced from their homes and that their possessions will still be there when they come home from work.[12] But Neuwirth's skepticism of Western-style property rights runs deep. He offers such quasi-Marxist assertions as: "When property becomes a commodity—simply a means of making money—we have begun the process that leads to homelessness and abandonment of the social contract to care for each other."

The most influential work about the new slums, the Peruvian economist Hernando de Soto's *The Mystery of Capital,* published in 2000, takes the ownership side of the debate, underscoring the limits of security of tenure. De Soto argues that the "surprise revolution"—the movement of millions from the countryside to cities—has been choked in its potential for uplift, not because slum dwellers lack talent or energy but because the legal systems in their new locales don't allow them to be secure in ownership and accumulate wealth. New arrivals in slums, de Soto explains, face "an impenetrable wall" of rules that bar them from "legally established social and economic activities."[13] Even when they begin to accumulate assets, those assets aren't safe. "Poor people save, but they hold these resources in defective forms: houses built on land whose ownership rights are not adequately recorded and unincorporated businesses with undefined liability." Without the formal legal institutions that allow one to accumulate wealth and borrow against it to build businesses, wealth cannot be put to full use, maintains de Soto. It stays locked up, frozen. It is "dead capital."

The logical solution, de Soto argues, is to bestow property on slum dwellers, a reform effort that has shown promise. A major "titling" program in Peru—the largest in the developing world— has issued 1.2 million property titles to poor urban households. The program has already had more immediate benefits: A study by the Harvard economist Erica Field concluded that it led to a "substantial increase in labor hours, a shift in labor supply away from work at home to work in the outside market and substitution of adult for child labor. For the average squatter family, granting of a property title is associated with a 17 percent increase in total household work hours... [and] a 28 percent reduction in the probability of child labor."

There are reasonable objections to titling. Is it fair for those who seized government land—or, worse, someone else's private property—to be rewarded with a property title? Nor is ownership easy to disentangle. "How do you allocate titles within the dense fabric of Rocinha or Kibera?" Neuwirth writes. "Who should get title to each parcel? The family that built the house? The woman who bought it from them? The tenants who rent there? The man who owns his two-story home but sold his roof rights to a friend, who built two stories and sold his roof rights to someone to build an additional two stories?"

Still, given the Peruvian evidence, it is dispiriting that the UN hasn't endorsed some kind of system of defined, enforceable property rights as a key to both slum improvement and overall economic development. Investing in improvements whose arbitrary loss they need not fear—and whose value they may someday capture through sale—can help slum dwellers move to bigger and better homes. And a property-rights regime isn't just about owner-occupied homes, either. One of the time-honored ways in which property rights support upward mobility is by allowing small landlords to acquire and maintain rental property as part of their own march toward affluence. A property-rights regime would be good, then, for both owners and renters in the slums.

Yet property rights and land title may not mean much in societies lacking developed financial institutions, including "mortgage lenders willing and able to go down market," as the FinMark Trust's Kecia Rust points out. And fostering those institutions—others include honest courts and a reliable and straightforward business-licensing process—is no simple matter. For mortgages, the value of slum buildings may not be well established, rendering them difficult to sell. Further, since many slum dwellers work in informal employment, their ability to repay home or business loans may not be obvious to potential lenders. But Habitat for Humanity has found proxies for a steady paycheck that can indicate a household's creditworthiness—regular payment of utility bills, say, and even regular church attendance.

The explosion of microfinance lending, which has extended capital markets to the very poor, also points a way. In Latin America, the nonprofit Acción Internacional has used a model in which neighbors vouch for one another and are liable collectively for missed payments.

Rust envisions a potentially bright housing picture. The owner of an extremely modest starter home might borrow a small amount to improve it as the first link in a chain of entrepreneurial activity, leading not only to ownership of a much larger home but to becoming "an investor, providing housing for other low-income earners" and earning "income for retirement." Already, the FinMark Trust has found, "small scale landlords provide accommodation for 1.85 million households across South Africa." This is a great leap forward from twentieth-century housing-reform thinking, which presumed that only external benevolence or government intervention and ownership could help slum dwellers.

Nevertheless, Rust's concern about the absence of reliable financial systems is a serious caution. Even if property rights are granted in the new slums, what will happen if such systems do not emerge? Mike Davis explores that dark scenario in his pessimistic *Planet of Slums*. In Davis's view, the emergent slums simply perpetuate inequality. "Their small businesses are a bare alternative to outright begging. Their hustle and bustle are a war of all against all, sparked by the oppressive Western economic prescriptions that have driven the Third World poor away from agriculture. And their denizens could provide the shock troops for an armed uprising, like the 1993 attacks on U.S. troops in Mogadishu by 'slum militias.'"

One wishes that such portrayals could be easily dismissed. But unless informal slum economies can be brought under the rule of law and integrated into broader national and global markets, the gloomier forecasts about the future of the slums may prove right. Above all, the developed world must not choke off the slums' already scant incomes by erecting trade barriers against the products of the developing world.

So the good news is that this generation's heirs to Jacob Riis seem to be avoiding the mistakes that he inspired. One piece of evidence that the popular view of slums (and slum dwellers) is changing: the surprise success of the film *Slumdog Millionaire* (2008), set in the shantytowns of Mumbai. Not only does the movie tell the story of the hero's rise from the bottom; his success—in a TV quiz show—is the result of what he's learned from the slums, not from school. A romantic view, true—it's a romantic movie—but also a long way from Riis.

Improving the world's new slums will require many institutions—Third World governments, international aid organizations, and Western nations and philanthropy—to get many policies right, from encouraging property rights to building a civil society to maintaining free trade. That, in the end, is what the slums—and we—must hope for.

Such efforts are, surprisingly, underway not just in the developing world but in the United States—on the Texas side of the Mexico border, where a sprawling network of small-town and rural "colonias" can be found. The Dallas Federal Reserve Bank, which has closely monitored these settlements, has estimated that "500,000 people live in 2,294 Texas colonias in Texas"—groups of homes that "may lack some of the most basic living necessities such as potable water, septic or sewer systems, electricity or safe and sanitary housing."[14] The modest homes, including trailers and many built by their own residents on small lots that they have purchased, are found in groups ranging from 40 to 300. Some are growing appendages to established cities such as Brownsville (reminiscent of South African townships outside major cities), in areas of "oil gas and cattle (and) mile upon miles of land of mesquite, cacti and dirt roads." Not all households are poor—but some 40 percent are so classified.

Yet, in keeping with the UN's contemporary approach to Third World urban slums, the Dallas Fed is surprisingly positive about the lives and prospects of colonia residents, some 73 percent of whom it finds to be U.S. citizens. Indeed, its 2015 overview report on the settlements is entitled "Las Colonias in the 21st Century: Progress Along the Texas-Mexico Border." "Commonly," concludes the Dallas Fed, based on interviews of residents, "the visible substandard conditions mask thriving communities in which neighbors support and provide for one another. This is why, despite high poverty rates, homelessness is rarely seen in the colonias." The report includes this comment by Ann Williams Cass of Projecto Azteca, an area homebuilder: "I find that people who live in the colonias are resilient, creative and not afraid of work. Some residents work two or three jobs in order to make ends meet." Williams notes—approvingly—that "you'll find two or three or four families living in one dwelling. They're just not going to let their relatives be left out."

Yet what some would call overcrowding and other aspects of colonia life have not sparked a return of the old housing reform impulses—demolition and clearance, replacement by publicly owned housing. Instead, the focus has been on improving the quality of life in the settlements as they exist. Between 2006 and 2014, the state of Texas "invested tens of millions of dollars in infrastructure projects," leading to "progress Texas colonias have made in building their infrastructure—including access to drinkable water, wastewater disposal, legal plats, paved roads, adequate drainage."

Notes the Dallas Fed, referring to a color-coded classification system it developed: "In 2006, 636 colonias were labeled green with access to drinkable water, adequate drainage, wastewater disposal, solid waste disposal, paved roads and legal plats. By 2014, an additional 286 colonias had access to all forms of infrastructure. In 2006, 396 colonias were labeled yellow with access only to drinkable water, wastewater disposal and legal plats; however, by 2014, 555 colonias were classified as yellow. There were 442 colonias having none of the most basic infrastructure (labeled red) in 2006, but by 2014 this number had dropped to 337." These changes represent appreciable overall progress. Indeed, some colonias have become incorporated municipalities with elected mayors and city councils—bringing their residents into the American polity with a direct capacity to shape decisions at the very local level.

In striking contrast to the aftermath of demolition in the urban renewal era, individual home and land ownership is common—bringing with it growth in household financial assets in ways that African Americans in Black Bottom, Detroit, were denied.

These modest, often self-built latter-day Levittowns range widely in quality—"from substandard to well-built: hybrid dwellings that are a combination of a recreational vehicle or trailer home with a wooden or cinder block addition, pier and beam homes, cinder block homes and standard brick or stucco homes on cement foundations."

But owned homes—both single-family and multifamily—are understood to be the standard. "In the Mexican culture, you have not lived until you have your little piece of land," observes David Arizmendi of South Texas College. "It is your identity, it is who you are...in a colonia, the process of homeownership begins with the purchase of a small plot of land to say, 'The land I'm stepping on is mine' is referred to as the American Dream."[15] There is reason for concern, however, as to whether homes that colonia residents believe to be their own actually are. It is not uncommon for residents to sign "contract-for-deed" arrangements under which they do not own property outright until they have made required monthly payments for the duration of the contract (up to twenty-five years). Failure to make a payment leads to forfeiture of the property. A 2016 Pew Charitable Trust study of the practice has referred to it as "the underbelly of American real estate."[16] It includes this example:

> To Freddie McKinney, buying the mobile home seemed like a great idea. It was big enough for McKinney, his wife and his elderly mother. The fenced eight-acre property in Harwood, Texas, was perfect for their dogs and horses. McKinney only had to pay $500 to move in, two years ago, with the understanding that after paying the developer $1,000 a month for twenty-five years, he'd own the property.
>
> At least, he says, that was the plan. Now the developer is demanding McKinney pay back taxes owed under the contract—money 68-year-old McKinney says he shouldn't have to pay—and county officials say the entire subdivision may be illegal.
>
> McKinney has a "contract for deed," a financing arrangement common in some low-income communities that can leave home-buyers in a legal mess.

The trends in home and land values in the colonias have been the subject of scholarly analysis, notably by a research team led by Peter Ward of the Lyndon B. Johnson School of Public Affairs at the University of Texas. Ward describes a housing market replete with both legal and illegal land sales and finds both resident and absentee owners, and concludes that even holding legal land title is no assurance of increasing home wealth. In other words, life in the colonias must not be sugar-coated. Nonetheless, Ward concludes that "the bootstraps approach and the self-managed opportunities for home-ownership in colonias and similar sub-divisions in the U.S. do offer important positive outcomes as place of residence as well as providing a mechanism for saving and creating equity."[17]

This is not to say that there are not those promoting the idea of some form of subsidized "affordable" housing in the colonias. But even these groups emphasize the local residents' preference for home ownership—and see any subsidies as modest sums meant to provide homes of a size or type buyers would not otherwise be able to afford.[18] The Community Development Corporation of Brownsville (Texas), for instance, estimates that its typical colonia buyer needs a $10,000 subsidy from either a public or private source in order to finance a new home, which typically costs $85,000. This is the same approach as that of the Nehemiah program—an emphasis on ownership of both land and home, rather than public ownership and management, as the original housing reformers envisioned when they conceived of housing, broadly, as a sort of public utility. That even the arguably Riis-like conditions of the colonias would not revive such a worldview says much about the retreat from housing reform.

Ironically, one of the latter-day versions of the reform vision—costly new "affordable" housing financed through the Low Income Housing Tax Credit—is actually viewed as an obstacle by groups active in the colonia region because of reformer-style conditions attached to it. The emphasis on deconcentrating poverty encourages groups like that in Brownsville to find home sites outside the colonias, where land is more expensive and building may not be welcome.

"...the Rio Grande Valley's poverty presents issues in the tax credit world as well, as part of the state requirements include fair housing guidelines for prioritizing projects in 'high opportunity' neighborhoods. The problem is that the Valley's widespread poverty makes such an area extremely hard to find."[19] In other words, a federal housing program designed to assist the poor runs counter to the idea of improving the quality of life in one of the largest contemporary "slum" areas, one in which extended families live together and the bonds of community run deep.

In contrast, both the Dallas Federal Reserve and the United Nations are viewing the colonias and the slums of the developing world as places where the emphasis must be on making poor communities better communities. They reflect an implicit view that we must avoid extrapolating from a snapshot of current conditions and concluding, as did early twentieth-century housing reformers, that such conditions were both inevitable and permanent. Instead, poor neighborhoods can be understood as places where ambition takes form, places that serve as repositories of financial assets that help make upward mobility possible.

At the same time, it's important that there also be homes and communities to which the poor can plausibly aspire to move up. That goal brings us back to the obstacles posed by zoning and to an even broader question: how to exorcise the housing reform impulse.

CHAPTER XI

Unreforming Housing

There are two intertwining themes in this book.

First, how to understand and, if possible, minimize or eliminate the distortions that the housing reform movement has, over the past generations, introduced into housing markets and the patterns of neighborhood residential life in America.

Second, how to take steps that will restore what was lost—a spectrum of housing and neighborhood types in American communities generally, not just to serve the need for shelter but to introduce a healthy, not artificial socioeconomic diversity into our civic life.

It is admittedly a daunting task. Careers and specialties have been built on the frameworks established by housing reform. These include those who work for public housing authorities, act as attorneys for tax credit deals, or, in the case of housing policy research centers, enjoy appointments as faculty members at Harvard, New York University, the University of California, Berkeley, and elsewhere. Social scientists devote themselves to analyzing the impact of various housing policies. The Department of Housing and Urban Development itself has more than 8,000 employees among its 10 regional offices and Washington headquarters. There are 3,400 public housing authorities in large cities and small towns across the U.S. The New York City Housing Authority alone has more than 10,000 employees. Housing developers have learned to specialize in building "affordable" housing, with its own specialized applications, accounting, and ongoing subsidy systems, often built on ties to public officials. Non-profit developers reliant on financing construction through the sale of tax credits have become an "industry." Such needs have led to the development of specialized financial intermediaries, such as the New York–based Local Initiatives Support Corporation, a non-profit community development financial institution (CDFI) that supports community development initiatives in 35 cities and across 2,100 rural counties in 44 states—and specializes in the syndication of housing tax credits.

Change—what I'm calling "unreform"—will have to come to all this incrementally, just as this policy apparatus was incrementally built. But even modest policy changes can be consequential.

Such changes should start with the ambition-killing rules that govern "affordable" housing. Residents of public and other forms of subsidized housing in the U.S. must be permitted to pay a flat rent set in a lease—rather than paying 30 percent of their income in rent and thus discouraging both earning more, marriage, and even such traditional expedients as taking in boarders to occupy empty bedrooms. (An estimated 25 percent of New York City public housing households actually have more bedrooms than residents and are known as "over-housed.")

New tenants should agree to short-term leases—say, the same five-year limit that's attached to cash public assistance. Public and subsidized housing can become a way station, not a way of life. Such an approach has already been taken by a small number of public housing authorities included in a HUD program called Moving to Work, which allows authorities to experiment with their own rules. The San Bernardino, California, Housing Authority, for instance, is one of twenty that have adopted time limits for new tenants. The Authority's language is notably different than that of Catherine Bauer or Edith Elmer Wood. In explaining why new housing voucher–holders face a time limit: "The goal of the activity is to enable the families we serve to focus on self-sufficiency efforts while we assist them with their housing needs for a limited term."[1] The head of the San Bernardino Housing Authority, Daniel J. Nackerman, said this about its five-year time limit program in Congressional testimony in 2013:

"This 5-year strategy is a bold initiative that changes the premise that once a person is in the program, they get to stay forever. It makes space on our waiting lists. It has kind of a life coach and counselor for each resident entering the program. And it really is helping to advance the quality of life of the persons we serve."[2] More specifically, as the Authority has put it, "In 2019, a total of 212 families transitioned to self-sufficiency through our activities."[3] This in a public housing system that includes just over 1,000 apartments and distributes some 7,700 housing vouchers.

The goal of converting public housing from a de facto poorhouse to a role as a transition to upward mobility—changing the culture, in the process, from one of dependency and despondency to one of hope and aspiration—is not implausible. In the nation's largest public housing system, that of New York City, a 2019 report found that, although a majority of tenants stayed more than five years, a significant group did not. The idea of encouraging more to move up and out is, thus, not implausible.

Household Length of Stay in NYCHA

Year Moved in to NYCHA	Number of Households Moved In	Still in NYCHA as of 1/1/2019	
		NUMBER	PERCENTAGE[4]
2009	7,255	4,624	64%
2014	5,913	4,704	80%

Source: New York City Housing Authority, Performance Tracking and Analytics Department, Tenant Data System 2009, 2014, and 2019.

It's even worth considering what might be called public housing "reparations"—financial buyouts of long-term public housing tenants—in recognition of the fact that many were steered into the projects when they were new and well kept. Housing reform effectively directed them away from asset ownership and the lifetime accumulation of wealth. This was especially true for African Americans, as in the tragic story of Black Bottom. Blacks arrived in large numbers in urban areas at the same time that policy housing construction was reaching its zenith—and they were arguably herded into projects especially reserved for them, as in Detroit. This was reflected in the fact that public housing was often named for heroic and accomplished African Americans: Ida B. Wells, Langston Hughes, Frederick Douglass, even James Weldon Johnson, the author of "Lift Every Voice and Sing," the so-called "Negro National Anthem." Its inspirational lyrics are in sharp contrast to life in the project named for Johnson in East Harlem.

Sing a song full of the faith that the dark past has taught us
Sing a song full of the hope that the present has brought us
Facing the rising sun of our new day begun
Let us march on 'til victory is won.

The broad goal of unreform must be this: The projects and "affordable" buildings themselves must gradually be absorbed into the private market. This should not be considered impractical. Since 2013, a HUD program called the Rental Assistance Demonstration has transferred management of public housing developments to private firms. Over time, this can become the means through which the "projects" become wholly private. A transition must be carefully thought through, in deference to the low incomes and long tenures of many tenants. But buyouts—or reparations—can be a means to helping tenants vacate such complexes, which might be cleared for new uses in their cities. Just as single-family zoning has "frozen" suburban land use patterns, so, too, has public and other forms of subsidized housing frozen urban land use. In New York City, there are more than 300 individual housing projects. They sit on land area equivalent to 150 sites the size of the World Trade Center complex, including valuable sites on the city's waterfront and in other high-value areas. The sale of such assets, with a requirement that a portion of the proceeds be directed to tenants, could ease the transition away from public housing. So, too, can public housing "campuses" be normalized by linking them to their surrounding cities by criss-crossing them with new streets on which new private homes, stores, and businesses could front.

The income inequities that characterize American society, like its industrialized counterparts, will always call out for some sorts of financial support for the poorest and other transfer payments to the working poor. But it is folly to channel such safety net supports through a costly system of publicly owned or publicly subsidized housing—which serves a minority of those judged eligible for such help based on their income.[5] Housing reform has led to vast distortions—in the incentives for low-income households to accumulate assets and improve their station, in the land use regulation of middle-class areas wary of the historical record of subsidized projects. Crucially, what's more, housing reform has undermined the development of healthy low-income neighborhoods, including poorer sides of wealthy towns—places where modest homes and small businesses are owned and occupied by their residents.

Changing all this would be, to be sure, a difficult process, complicated by groups that promote the idea that, because many Americans pay more than a third of their income in rent, more and more subsidized housing is required.[6] Such assertions overlook the fact that housing reform policies actually work to create the situation they purport to correct—by discouraging multi-generational and two-parent households and penalizing gains in personal income.

Nonetheless, if public housing and its latter-day reform variations are to be phased out, there must also be complementary efforts to restore the "tenement trail" out of the poorest neighborhoods and into analogues of Brookline's historic Farm, a mix of what can be called "naturally occurring affordable housing": two- and three-family homes, some with storefronts, that are part of larger communities comprising neighborhoods of various income groups.

Such an aspiration leads, inevitably, back to the biggest distortion in American housing markets, one as deleterious in its own way as public housing: single-family zoning, the most widespread residue of Progressive era housing reform.

This, too, is a daunting task. It is folly, however, to believe it will be achieved through racialized attacks on "exclusionary" jurisdictions, relying on the heavy hand of the federal or state government. As the backlash in Forest Hills was the first to make clear, that is the route to maximum political resistance. Instead, zoning reform—a movement away from single-family zoning as the default—will have to be realized through political persuasion.

That, after all, was the way that zoning came to be—through the city-by-city persuasion of Lawrence Veiller, the Johnny Appleseed of zoning, and his minions in the Housing Betterment Association. Veiller hit the road to persuade and came ready with a model zoning law for local officials to adopt—and they did.

What would be the arguments of a contemporary Veiller, chastened by what he had wrought and seeking to persuade today's local officials to make adjustments? In answering that question, it's important to examine initiatives that are, once again, proving to be counterproductive.

Among the best examples of a counterproductive approach is that of Minneapolis, which, in 2019, gained national prominence for a citywide plan that actually ended single-family zoning. The *New York Times* spotlighted the plan for daring to "question an American ideal: a house with a yard on every lot."[7] "We're all hoping for Minneapolis to succeed," said a representative of the National League of Cities in December 2019, at a Department of Housing and Urban Development conference in Washington.[8]

But, following the same pattern that began in Forest Hills decades earlier, the plan stirred backlash—in no small part because it was cast by its proponents less as a means to provide more housing opportunities than as recompense for alleged racial injustice.

The leading voice of Minneapolis rezoning was City Council President Lisa Bender, a onetime San Francisco city planner elected to a position that many consider more powerful than the city's mayoralty, now that young Progressives have replaced five incumbents on the thirteen-member council. She and other proponents cast the plan not just as a housing reform, over which compromise might be found, but as a necessary means of undoing deep-rooted racial injustice. "We've inherited a system that both for decades has privileged those with the most and forgotten the people that we really have left behind," Bender said. "And housing is inextricably linked with income, with all these other systems that are failing, especially in Minnesota, people of color."[9] Rather than trying to persuade the affluent that relaxed zoning regulations might be in their interest, should they wish someday to downsize; or in the interest of their adult children, looking for affordable places to live in the city; or beneficial to Minneapolis's overall economic future, Minneapolis Progressives racialized the housing issue. A newspaper editorial saw the plan as a corrective to "special benefits made available over time to the white population." They referred to federal mortgage guidelines, such as those in force in the early years of Levittown, that had, indeed, hampered Blacks' ability to buy homes. Radical corrective action was therefore needed to expand lower-income housing—especially in affluent, predominantly (though by no means exclusively) white neighborhoods.

The zoning change was, although widely publicized, largely symbolic. Like most older Northeast and Midwest cities, Minneapolis already contained a mixture of single-family homes, two-family homes, and small and mid-sized apartment buildings. What's more, high land values in more affluent areas made it unlikely that development of lower-cost housing in such areas would occur, even after zoning relaxation. But the 2040 plan proved important, nonetheless—in a way that should serve as a warning for those seeking to ease the single-family zoning freeze.

The plan prompted organized opposition, both among African American groups who felt that historically low-income Black neighborhoods, and the city's public housing, would not be helped by it—and among homeowners in more affluent parts of the city who were concerned that apartment blocks would rise on blocks otherwise dotted with craftsmen's cottages. Census data, moreover, showed that African Americans were well represented, as predicted by their incomes, in even the most affluent sections of the city.[10] Nonetheless, opposition to the plan wound up being vilified at a public hearing as "white pastoralism." Such attacks stunned middle-class homeowners, many of whom considered themselves left liberals. Predictably, legal action to halt the plan on environmental grounds was initiated.

But the danger sparked by the controversy goes beyond what will happen in Minneapolis. It demonstrates the danger of tying zoning change to larger, hot-button issues such as race, when doing so risks alienating, not persuading, the thousands of local planning and zoning boards across the U.S. in whom the actual power to relax zoning lies. Steve Cramer, head of the Minneapolis Downtown Council and a former Minneapolis city council member, observes, "There's been a 'blaming and shaming' aspect of the discussion, which didn't adequately separate historical decisions and motivations which had discriminatory intent from the current-day reality of homeowners who have invested in their property and neighborhood, and now were being found guilty by association with the past.[11]

Those who would unlock American zoning must bear in mind that there are more than 19,000 independent municipalities in the U.S. with the power to adopt plans and zoning to implement those plans. What's more, it is suburban and exurban areas where change would have to occur. Minneapolis, for instance, is not a bastion of single-family homeowners, as reformers suggest. According to census data, single-family homes account for only 42.9 percent of residential structures in the city. A mix of row houses and two- to nine-family structures make up another 20 percent, with the remainder comprising units in larger apartment buildings. The city—much of it built in the pre-zoning era—is already a model of mixed residential housing, in other words. Outlying, affluent Minneapolis suburbs are not affected by the city's restrictions on single-family zoning and potentially alienated by the arguments made for it. A prime example: Affluent Shorewood, Minnesota, a postwar suburb where what limited zoning variation there is consists mainly in establishing lot sizes for single-family homes—ranging from big (10,000 square feet) to bigger (20,000 square feet).[12]

The question, then, is how, as a matter of political persuasion, to bring housing unreform to the thousands of American municipalities frozen to permit the single-family home or nothing at all. Asking—or ordering—such jurisdictions to accept subsidized low-income housing may appear to be a "social justice" initiative—but is not only likely to spark opposition but risks relegating potential low-income beneficiaries to small de facto subsidized reservations—the newest versions of public housing—without the sort of lively communities and social fabric in the Farm or Black Bottom tradition. On a visit to homes built as part of an "inclusionary" zoning program in affluent Montgomery County, Maryland (suburban Washington, DC), low-income residents told me of taking multiple buses into the city each weekend in order to attend church in the communities from which they had relocated.

But if zoning coercion is counterproductive, how might "unfreezing" take place? The most promising emerging approach emphasizes the need to fill in what's called the "missing middle." In 2015, the mayor of Seattle convened a housing task force and charged it with finding ways to build 30,000 new homes by 2025. The task force concluded that the city was "constrained by outdated policies and historical precedents," such as single-family zoning of two-thirds of Seattle's land. The committee proposed significant upzonings (changes to permit greater density) to allow new multifamily construction—including designating 6 percent of single-family areas for low-rise multifamily construction, as well as raising height limits in existing multifamily areas toward a 75-foot "sweet spot," which would produce the lowest construction cost per unit.

The idea appears particularly promising because it has attracted more than theoretical support. The National Association of Home Builders, the nationwide trade group, specifically promotes it. Missing middle housing, as defined by writer and architect Daniel Parolek, is "a range of multi-unit or clustered housing types, compatible in scale with detached single-family homes."[13] For Parolek, such housing is "called 'middle' for two reasons: because of its scale and because of its ability to deliver affordability to middle-income households. Whether in urban or suburban locations, these types of homes can take many forms, including bungalow courts, townhomes, duplexes or triplexes and courtyard apartments."[14]

Such are the rungs of a ladder of housing types that allow households to both afford shelter and accumulate wealth. The "missing middle" argument has the advantage of dovetailing with contemporary conventional wisdom that the American middle class is "vanishing." Absent the fear engendered by "low-income housing," "missing middle" proposals can—accurately—be portrayed to local planning and zoning boards as a way for younger households to find "starter homes" in the towns where they grew up—and to provide a next generation of buyers for older homeowners as they retire and perhaps even downsize to a smaller missing middle home type. The missing middle can include so-called "accessory dwelling units"—second housing units built on the lots of existing houses—that can serve as rental units or "in-law apartments" or "granny flats." Zoning entire neighborhoods for such housing would, in one fell swoop, make for a new unsubsidized but "affordable" area—in which homebuyers could become small landlords and help pay their mortgage loans. Such "ADUs" have become more common in recent years. San Jose, California, for instance, where single-family homes comprise 65 percent of the housing stock, has seen the number of applications for the required permits rise dramatically.[15] But lot-by-lot zoning change is slow and burdensome. Far better to rezone a larger area—in effect, making it into an opportunity zone.

Similarly, neighborhoods can be "upzoned" en masse from single-family to two-family, permitting existing buildings to be converted. In other words, there's no need to abolish all single-family zoning across a city or town in order to fill the missing middle. Incremental change—far more likely to gain political acceptance—would matter.

In the Lawrence Veiller tradition, the missing middle idea is one that can be promoted by municipal groups such as the National League of Cities, the National Association of Counties, or the National Association of Towns and Townships—as well as by home-builder groups. Even the federal Department of Housing and Urban Development could provide model zoning proposals instead of trying to unfreeze the suburbs through the threat of cutting off streams of federal assistance. Small homes on small lots are the next step up the housing ladder for those leaving public housing—just as the Reverend Johnny Ray Youngblood and builder I.D. Robbins demonstrated in their Nehemiah Homes.

The addition of a range of new housing and neighborhood types injected into the frozen zoning and planning maps of America should not be understood as a complement to dispersed public and subsidized housing. It's a full-blown alternative. It embodies persuasion rather than coercion. Its message is a positive one—one that can plausibly influence the tens of thousands of local zoning board officials, many of them volunteers whose felt obligation is to their neighbors, not to abstract ideas about affordability and social justice. They will have to be convinced that a move away from large-lot single-family zoning is in the interest of those whom they serve. "Missing middle" housing—privately built and unsubsidized—should be seen as a substitute for the reform projects that have distorted housing markets, skewed the incentives of lower-income families, denied the poor the opportunity to accumulate assets, and leveled historic and vibrant poor sides of town, leaving sterility and despair behind.

It is time—long past time—to turn our backs on housing reform. It is time for housing unreform.

Or, as as the pop singer Johnny Rivers once memorably put it, "Together we can make it, baby, from the poor side of town."

NOTES

INTRODUCTION: THE NEIGHBORHOODS WE'VE LOST AND THE ONES WE NEED

1 Keith N. Morgan, "Brookline Comprehensive Plan, 2005-2015," Society of Architectural Historians Archipedia, https://www.brooklinema.gov/DocumentCenter/View/246/Community-Facilities?bidId=; https://sah-archipedia.org/buildings/MA-01-BR28.

2 Heliotype Printing Co., "Map of the Estate of the Brookline Land Company and Vicinity, 42 x 89 cm." (1892), Digital Commonwealth, accessed November 12, 2020, https://www.digitalcommonwealth.org/search/commonwealth:1257bc81v.

3 In Canada and throughout Europe, public housing is termed "social housing."

CHAPTER I: JACOB RIIS AND THE REFORMER'S GAZE

1 Tom Buk-Swienty, *The Other Half: The Life of Jacob Riis and the World of Immigrant America*, trans. Annette Buk-Swienty (New York: W. W. Norton & Company, 2008), 143.

2 Ibid. 142.

3 Ibid. 143.

4 Ibid. 167–168, 173.

5 Jacob A. Riis, *How the Other Half Lives* (Project Gutenberg, 2014), chap. 4, 28, https://www.gutenberg.org/files/45502/45502-h/45502-h.htm.

6 Buk-Swienty, *The Other Half*, 210.

7 Ibid. 255.

8 Friedrich Engels, *The Condition of the Working-Class in England in 1844 with Preface Written in 1892*, trans. by Florence Kelley Wischnewetzky (London: Swan Sonnenschein & Co., 1887).

9 Irving Howe, *World of Our Fathers: The Journey of the East European Jews to America and the Life They Found and Made* (New York and London: Harcourt, Brace, Jovanovich, 1976), 119–120.

10 Buk-Swienty, *The Other Half*, 173.

11 Ibid.

CHAPTER II: THE ZONE OF EMERGENCE

1 Michael Minn, "326 Rivington Street Public Bath," accessed November 20, 2020, http://michaelminn.net/newyork/research/public-baths/rivington-street/index.html.

2 "Tenement House Reform," VCU Libraries Social Welfare History Project, accessed October 20, 2020, https://socialwelfare.library.vcu.edu/issues/poverty/tenement-house-reform/.

3 U.S. Bureau of Labor and Commissioner of Labor Carroll D. Wright, *The Slums of Baltimore, Chicago, New York, and Philadelphia*, special report prepared in compliance with a joint resolution of the Congress, Bureau of Labor, July 1892, 11–19.

4 C. Osborn, "The Slums of Great Cities," *Economic Journal* 5, no. 19 (1895): 474–476, doi:10.2307/2955646.

5 Wright, *The Slums of Baltimore, Chicago, New York, and Philadelphia*, 19.

6 U.S. Bureau of Labor and Commissioner of Labor Carroll D. Wright, *Slums in Great Cities*, special report prepared for Congress, Bureau of Labor, 1894.

7 U.S. Immigration Commission and William P. Dillingham, *Immigrants in the United States*, published as Senate documents of the 61st Congress (Washington, D.C., 1907–1910).

8 Wright, *Slums in Great Cities*.

9 Olivier Zunz, *The Changing Face of Inequality: Urbanization, Industrial Development and Immigrants in Detroit, 1880–1920* (Chicago: University of Chicago Press, 1982).

10 Robert A. Woods and Albert J. Kennedy, *The Zone of Emergence: Observations of the Lower Middle and Upper Working Class Communities of Boston, 1905–1914* (Massachusetts: MIT Press, 1962), 39.

11 Woods and Kennedy, *The Zone of Emergence*, 19.

12 U.S. Census Bureau, *Census of Population and Housing, 1940*, Table 75, Housing General Characteristics.

13 "Why Are Bungalows Prevalent in the East Bay and What Defines the Style?" Berkeley Hills Realty, last modified September 21, 2016, https://berkhills.com/bay-area-living/bungalows-prevalent-east-bay-defines-style/.

14 "Research Your Shaker Home," Shaker Heights Homes, last modified October 17, 2020, https://shakerlibrary.org/local-history/research/homes/.

15 Helen L. Parrish, "One Million People in Small Houses—Philadelphia," The Housing Awakening Series Part IX, Survey 26, no. 6 (May 1911).

16 George Orwell, *The Road to Wigan Pier* (New York: Houghton Mifflin Harcourt, 1958), 52.

17 Roy Lubove, "Lawrence Veiller and the New York State Tenement House Commission of 1900," *Journal of American History* 47, no. 4 (March 1961), 659–667. Veiller, in the aftermath of the publication of *How the Other Half Lives*, also served as secretary of the New York State Tenement House Commission and First Deputy Tenement Commissioner of the Tenement Department of New York City.

18 Lawrence Veiller, *A Model Housing Law* (New York: Russell Sage Foundation second edition, 1920), 13, https://www.russellsage.org/sites/default/files/Veiller_Model_Housing_Law_0.pdf.

19 "The Urban Log Cabin," Thirteen, accessed October 27, 2020 https://www.thirteen.org/tenement/logcabin.html. The term was used as part of the promotion for a public television film about the museum.

20 Lillian Wald, *The House on Henry Street*, (New York: Henry Holt and Company, 1915), 46.

21 U.S. Congress, *An Act to regulate the immigration of aliens to, and the residence of aliens in, the United States*, HR 103084, Sixty-Fourth Cong., 2nd sess., approved February 5, 1917, https://www.loc.gov/law/help/statutes-at-large/64th-congress/session-2/c64s2ch29.pdf.

22 Neil Swidey, "Trump's Anti-Immigration Playbook Was Written 100 Years Ago. In Boston," *Boston Globe*, January 2017, https://apps.bostonglobe.com/magazine/graphics/2017/01/immigration/.

23 Prescott F. Hall, "The Menace of the Three-Decker," *Housing Betterment* (January 1917), 38, https://books.google.com/books?id=k3XseuvXkKoC&pg=RA6-PT3.

CHAPTER III: "MODERN HOUSING"
AND THE CRUSADE AGAINST THE POOR SIDE

1 Howard Husock, "The Tragic Lessons of Urban Renewal at Brookline's Farm," *Boston Globe*, January 31, 2020, https://www.bostonglobe.com/2020/01/31/opinion/tragic-lessons-urban-renewal-brooklines-farms/.

2 Elaine Latzman Moon, *Untold Tales, Unsung Heroes: An Oral History of Detroit's African-American Community, 1918–1967* (Detroit: Wayne State University Press, 1994).

3 Edith Abbott Wood, "A Century of the Housing Problem," Columbia University, Papers of Edith Abbott Wood, Miscellaneous Papers, Box 67, Folder 5.

4 Brookline Redevelopment Authority, *The Farm Redevelopment Project: Project no. UR Mass 15-1* (Brookline: The Authority, 1957), https://find.minlib.net/iii/encore/record/C___Rb1782634.

5 Author's research based on U.S. Census, 1950, For Underlying data, see Appendix A.

6 U.S. Department of Commerce, *Bureau of the Census, St. Louis, Missouri Census Tracts*, "Table 3, Characteristics of Dwelling Units by Census Tracts," 52. This source is used throughout.

7 Calculations at the request of the author based on U.S. Census, 1950.

8 Nathan Glazer, *From a Cause to a Style*, Princeton University Press, 2007, 51.

9 Ashley Holder and Molly Calvo, "Extant Buildings in the Mill Creek Valley: Past, Present and Future," Decoding the City, accessed October 27, 2020, http://www.decodingstl.org/extant-buildings-in-the-mill-creek-valley-past-present-and-future/. "(Undated) The Dixie Cream building itself was actually spared the wrecker's ball and, in the 21st century, would house tech start-up businesses."

10 Peter H. Rossi and Robert A. Dentler, *The Politics of Urban Renewal* (New York: Macmillan, 1961).

11 "Black Bottom Neighborhood," Detroit Historical Society, accessed October 27, 2020 https://detroithistorical.org/learn/encyclopedia-of-detroit/black-bottom-neighborhood.

12 "Edith Elmer Wood Papers, 1900–1943," Columbia University Archives, accessed November 23, 2020, http://www.columbia.edu/cu/lweb/archival/collections/ldpd_3460606/.

13 "Wood, Edith Elmer," Encyclopedia, accessed October 27, 2020, https://www.encyclopedia.com/women/encyclopedias-almanacs-transcripts-and-maps/wood-edith-elmer-1871-1945.

14 "The Urban Log Cabin," Thirteen, accessed October 27, 2020 https://www.thirteen.org/tenement/logcabin.html.

15 Howard Husock, "'Re-streeting' the Projects," *City Journal*, Spring 2019, https://www.city-journal.org/integrating-nycha-surrounding-communities.

16 Catherine Bauer, *Modern Housing* (Minneapolis: University of Minnesota Press, 1934), 136.

17 Jean-Louis Cohen, *Le Corbusier and the Mystique of the USSR: Theories and Projects for Moscow, 1928–1936* (Princeton: Princeton University Press, 1992).

18 Central Intelligence Agency, *Housing Policies in the Soviet Union*, February 1955, https://www.cia.gov/library/readingroom/docs/OGATA%2C%20TAKETORA%20%20%20VOL.%201_0006.pdf.

19 Kyle Norris, "Here's Why the Brewster-Douglass Housing Projects Were Built in the 1930s," Michigan Radio, March 17, 2015, www.michiganradio.org/post/here-s-why-brewster-douglass-housing-projects-were-built-1930s.

20 Bauer was named Director of Information and Research for the newly formed United States Housing Authority, which served as the vehicle for public borrowing to finance the construction of public housing; she wrote the landmark National Housing Act of 1937, which, as amended, has continued to serve as the basis for all housing subsidized by the U.S. federal government; Wood served in both the Public Works Administration and the U.S. Housing Authority: Vassar Encyclopedia, Catherine Bauer Wurster: http://vcencyclopedia.vassar.edu/alumni/Catherine%20Bauer%20Wurster.html.

21 P.G. Watkins (director, Black Bottom Archives), in discussion with the author, July 23, 2020.

22 "This Is What We Do," Black Scroll Network, accessed October 27, 2020 https://blackscrollnetwork.weebly.com/.

23 "Black Bottom Neighborhood," Detroit Historical Society, accessed October 27, 2020 https://detroithistorical.org/learn/encyclopedia-of-detroit/black-bottom-neighborhood.

24 Richard Rothstein, "Public Works Administration: Term Analysis," The Color of Law, LitCharts, accessed October 27, 2020, https://www.litcharts.com/lit/the-color-of-law/terms/public-works-administration-pwa.

25 "Harold Ickes Homes," Chicago Gang History, accessed October 27, 2020, https://chicagoganghistory.com/housing-project/harold-ickes-homes/.

26 Nathan Glazer, "West End Story," *New York Review*, February 1, 1963.

27 Herbert Gans, *The Urban Villagers: Group and Class in the Life of Italian-Americans* (New York: The Free Press, 1962), 351–352.

28 Alex Kotlowitz, *There Are No Children Here: The Story of Two Boys Growing Up in the Other America* (New York: Random House, 1991).

29 Jon Pynoos, Robert Schafer, and Chester W. Hartman, *Housing Urban America* (London: Aldine Publishing Co., 1980), 474.

30 "Pruitt–Igoe," Wikipedia, https://en.wikipedia.org/wiki/Pruitt%E2%80%93Igoe.

31 Lee Rainwater, *Behind Ghetto Walls: Life in a Federal Slum* (Chicago: Transaction Publishers, 1970), 3–5.

32 Howard Husock, "The Myths of the Pruitt-Igoe Myth," *City Journal*, February 17, 2012, https://www.city-journal.org/html/myths-pruitt-igoe-myth-9698.html.

33 *Shelley v. Kraemer*, 334 U.S. 1 (1948).

34 Thomas J. Sugrue, *The Origins of the Urban Crisis* (Princeton: Princeton University Press, 2005), 73–75.

35 Allida M. Black, "Eleanor Roosevelt and the Wartime Campaign against Jim Crow," accessed November 6, 2020, http://www.socialstudies.org/sites/default/files/publications/se/6005/600508.html.

36 Ken Coleman, "Detroit's Black Bottom and Paradise Valley, What Happened?" Detroitisit, October 5, 2017, https://detroitisit.com/black-bottom-and-paradise-valley-communities/.

37 "Major Legislation on Housing and Urban Development Enacted Since 1932," U.S. Department of Housing and Urban Development, accessed November 6, 2020, https://www.hud.gov/sites/documents/LEGS_CHRON_JUNE2014.PDF.

38 Dan Austin, "Meet the 5 Worst Mayors in Detroit History," *Detroit Free Press*, August 29, 2014, https://www.freep.com/story/news/local/2014/08/29/5-worst-mayors-in-detroit-history/14799541/.

39 Richard Rothstein, *The Color of Law: The Forgotten History of How Our Government Segregated America* (New York: W. W. Norton, 2017), 64.

CHAPTER IV: "YES, YES. WE WEREN'T DREAMING":
THE TRIUMPH OF LEVITTOWN

1 Nitin Nohria, Anthony Mayo, and Mark Benson, "William Levitt, Levittown and the Creation of American Suburbia," *Harvard Business School Case Collection*, December 2005 (revised March 2010), https://www.hbs.edu/faculty/Pages/item.aspx?num=32887.

2 Witold Rybczynski, "Living Smaller," *Atlantic*, February 1991, https://www.theatlantic.com/magazine/archive/1991/02/living-smaller/306205/.

3 Nohria, Mayo, and Benson, "William Levitt, Levittown and the Creation of American Suburbia."

4 Herbert J. Gans, *The Levittowners: Ways of Life and Politics in a New Suburban Community* (New York: Columbia University Press, 1967), 23.

5 Michael D. Ullman, "Household Deformation and the Rise and Permanence of Homelessness," unpublished manuscript reviewed by the author. Referenced here: https://www.nhipdata.org/contributors.

6 Nohria, Mayo, and Benson, "William Levitt, Levittown and the Creation of American Suburbia," 406–62.

7 Malvina Reynolds, *Little Boxes* (New York: Oak Publications, 1964).

8 Pete Seeger, "We Shall Overcome: The Complete Carnegie Hall Concert," recorded June 8, 1963, Columbia—C2K 45312.

9 Nohria, Mayo, and Benson, "William Levitt, Levittown and the Creation of American Suburbia."

10 Ibid.

11 Ibid.

12 Gans, *The Levittowners*, 170.

13 Marian Morton, "Deferring Dreams: Racial and Religious Covenants in Shaker Heights, Cleveland Heights and East Cleveland, 1925 to 1970," Teaching Cleveland Digital, February 27, 2010, http://teachingcleveland.org/deferring-dreams-racial-and-religious-covenants-in-shaker-heights-and-cleveland-heights-1925-to-1970-by-marian-morton/.

14 Correspondence with the author, November 1, 2017.

CHAPTER V: THE UNREFORMER AND HER LESSONS NOT LEARNED

1 Robert Kanigel, *Eyes on the Street: The Life of Jane Jacobs* (New York: Alfred A. Knopf, 2016), 130–131.

2 Ibid. 146.

3 Ibid. 153.

4 Fair Housing Act," U.S. Department of Justice, accessed November 20, 2020, https://www.justice.gov/crt/faousing-act-2. Section 804 of the Act defines unlawful housing discrimination in this way, among others: (a) To refuse to sell or rent after the making of a bona fide offer, or to refuse to negotiate for the sale or rental of, or otherwise make unavailable or deny, a dwelling to any person because of race, color, religion, sex, familial status, or national origin.

5 Howard Husock, "How Brooke Helped Destroy Public Housing," *Forbes*, January 8, 2015, https://www.forbes.com/sites/howardhusock/2015/01/08/how-senator-brooke-helped-destroy-public-housing/?sh=295ba9e13fc3.

6 Howard Husock, "Why New York's Public Housing Should Encourage Commercial Development," Manhattan Institute, October 2016, https://media4.manhattan-institute.org/sites/default/files/R-HH-1016.pdf

7 Jeanne R. Lowe, *Cities in a Race with Time: Progress and Poverty in America's Renewing Cities* (New York: Random House, 1967).

8 Peter Kihss, "'Benign Neglect' on Race Is Proposed by Moynihan," *New York Times*, March 1, 1970, https://www.nytimes.com/1970/03/01/archives/benign-neglect-on-race-is-proposed-by-moynihan-moynihan-urges.html.

9 Robert C. Weaver, "Goals of the Department of Housing and Urban Development," *Urban Affairs Quarterly* 2, no. 2 (December 1966), 3–7.

10 Robert Wood, "Obligations of an Affluent Society," Address to National Association of Social Workers, May 27, 1966.

11 Oscar Newman, *Defensible Space: Crime Prevention through Urban Design* (New York: MacMillan, 1973), 3.

12 For example, see the attached homes: "Municipal Housing Authority of Yonkers," Municipal Housing Authority for the City of Yonkers, accessed November 20, 2020, https://mhacy.org/.

13 Howard Husock, "Gem in the Ghetto," *Boston Phoenix*, July 4, 1976. The article describes the effect of buildings renovated under the terms of Section 236 of the National Housing Act, as amended in 1968. The 236 program provided financing below market rates and was coupled with so-called project-based rent subsidies that guaranteed rental income for developers while limiting the rent paid by tenants.

14 Irving Welfeld, *HUD Scandals* (New York and London: Routledge, 2017), 45.

15 Howard Husock, "Policy Analysis. No. 292: The Inherent Flaws of HUD," December 22, 1997, https://www.cato.org/sites/cato.org/files/pubs/pdf/pa-292.pdf.

16 *HUD Multifamily Repair and Foreclosure Policies: Hearing before a Subcommittee of the Committee on Government Operations*, 98th Cong. (1983), https://books.google.com/books?id=Jqe1wYUl3UMC&pg=PA78. Also see Howard Husock, "Gem in the Ghetto," *Boston Phoenix*, July 4, 1976.

17 Ginia Bellafante, "A Housing Solution Gone Awry," *New York Times*, June 1, 2013, https://www.nytimes.com/2013/06/02/nyregion/in-marcus-garvey-village-a-housing-solution-gone-awry.html.

18 Bellafante, "A Housing Solution Gone Awry."

19 *The Final Report of the National Commission on Severely Distressed Public Housing, A Report to the Congress and Secretary of Housing and Urban Development*, United States Department of Housing and Urban Development, Washington, D.C., August 1992, https://www.hud.gov/sites/documents/DOC_9836.PDF. In 2017, the Garvey complex would be renovated through a new round of subsidies.

20 Nicholas Dagen Bloom, *Public Housing That Worked: New York in the Twentieth Century* (Philadelphia: University of Pennsylvania Press, 2009).

21 Luis Ferré-Sadurní and Benjamin Weiser, "Judge Rejects Deal to Overhaul City's Public Housing," *New York Times*, November 14, 2018, https://www.nytimes.com/2018/11/14/nyregion/nycha-settlement-court-ruling.html.

22 Howard Husock, "Ending NYCHA's Dependence Trap: Making Better Use of New York's Public Housing," Manhattan Institute, September 19, 2019, https://www.manhattan-institute.org/making-nycha-more-efficient.

23 Howard Husock, "Three Steps to a Better NYCHA: Encourage Upward Mobility and Free Up Apartments to People on the Waitlist," *New York Daily News*, September 22, 2019, https://www.nydailynews.com/opinion/ny-oped-making-nycha-work-right-now-20190922-zlab6sbcdndvhbyrgf6h6qe2q4-story.html.

24 "Assisted Housing: National and Local," Office of Policy Development and

Research, accessed November 6, 2020, https://www.huduser.gov/portal/datasets/assthsg.html.

25 Kriston McIntosh, Emily Moss, Ryan Nunn, and Jay Shambaugh, "Examining the Black-white Wealth Gap," Brookings Institute, February 27, 2020, https://www.brookings.edu/blog/up-front/2020/02/27/examining-the-black-white-wealth-gap/.

26 Howard Husock, "How Government Fostered Housing Segregation," *Barron's*, September 30, 2017, https://www.barrons.com/articles/how-government-fostered-housing-segregation-1506747830.

27 Husock, "Ending NYCHA's Dependence Trap: Making Better Use of New York's Public Housing."

CHAPTER VI: THE MINISTER AND THE BUILDER

1 "You see the trouble that we're in. How Jerusalem lies in ruins with its gates burned. Come let us rebuild the wall of Jerusalem, so that we may no longer suffer disgrace." Quote from Rev. Youngblood from Samuel G. Freedman, *Upon This Rock: The Miracles of the Black Church* (New York: Harper Collins, 1993).

2 Ibid. 41.

3 Ibid. 332–333.

4 Howard Husock, "Fred Trump, Middle Class Hero," *City Journal*, October 9, 2018, https://www.city-journal.org/fred-trump-middle-class-hero-16218.html.

5 Wolfgang Saxon, "Lester Robbins, 90, Who Built Row Houses for Public Housing," *New York Times*, July 16, 1996, https://www.nytimes.com/1996/07/16/nyregion/lester-robbins-90-who-built-row-houses-for-public-housing.html.

6 Samuel G. Freedman, "Letting Go, Gradually, of a Life Embracing the Ministry," *New York Times*, July 10, 2009, https://www.nytimes.com/2009/07/11/us/11religion.html.

7 Lawrence Van Gelder, "I. D. Robbins Is Dead at 86; Pioneer in Low-Cost Homes," *New York Times*, July 4, 1996, https://www.nytimes.com/1996/07/04/nyregion/i-d-robbins-is-dead-at-86-pioneer-in-low-cost-homes.html.

8 Lee Stuart with John Heinmeier, "The Nehemiah Strategy," in *Making Housing Happen, 2nd Edition: Faith-Based Affordable Housing Models*, ed. Jill Suzanne Shook (Oregon: Cascade Books, 2012), https://books.google.com/books?id=1xZTAwAAQBAJ&pg=PA197.

9 "Affordable Housing," East Brooklyn Congregations, accessed November 6, 2020, http://ebc-iaf.org/content/affordable-housing.

10 Jake Mooney, "Living on the Edge: East New York & Bay Ridge Go Off Script," *CityLimits*, March 3, 2011, https://citylimits.org/2011/03/03/living-on-the-edge-east-new-york-bay-ridge-go-off-script/.

11 Alan S. Oser, "A Housing Program's Next Generation," *New York Times*, December 21, 1997, https://www.nytimes.com/1997/12/21/realestate/a-housing-program-s-next-generation.html.

12 Abigail Savitch-Lew, "Brownsville Plan Gains Momentum, Sparks Hope

and Anxiety," *CityLimits*, August 29, 2018, https://citylimits.org/2018/08/29/
brownsville-plan-gains-momentum-sparks-hope-and-anxiety/.

13 Howard Husock, "It's Time to Take Habitat for Humanity Seriously," *City Journal*, Summer 1995, https://www.city-journal.org/html/it%E2%80%99s-time-take-habitat-humanity-seriously-11949.html.

14 John Fraser Hart, Michelle J. Rhodes, and John T. Morgan, "The Unknown World of the Mobile Home," *Urban Geography* 25, no. 2 (2004): 187–188, doi: 10.2747/0272-3638.25.2.187.

CHAPTER VII: THE SEARCH FOR THE PHILOSOPHER'S STONE

1 Paul A. Jargowsky, "Architecture of Segregation: Civil Unrest, the Concentration of Poverty, and Public Policy," *Atavist*, accessed November 9, 2020 https://tcfdotorg.atavist.com/architecture-of-segregation.

2 "HOPE VI Data Compilation and Analysis," PD&R Edge: An Online Magazine, accessed November 9, 2020, https://www.huduser.gov/portal/pdredge/pdr-edge-research-032017.html.

3 "Hope VI and Neighborhood Revitalization: Final Report," The Urban Institute, accessed November 9, 2020, https://www.urban.org/sites/default/files/publication/46711/411544-HOPE-VI-and-Neighborhood-Revitalization.PDF.

4 Chicago Housing Authority, *Oakwood Shores Redevelopment Plan*, March 2018, https://cha-assets.s3.us-east-2.amazonaws.com/s3fs-public/Oakwood%20Shores%20FINAL%20Document.pdf.

5 "Oakwood Shores," Chicago Housing Authority, accessed November 9, 2020, https://www.thecha.org/residents/public-housing/find-public-housing/oakwood-shores.

6 "Oakwood Shores," ApartmentRatings, accessed November 9, 2020, https://www.apartmentratings.com/il/chicago/oakwood-shores_9199332346275149291/.

7 Chris Edwards and Vanessa Brown Calder, "Low-Income Housing Tax Credit: Costly, Complex, and Corruption-Prone," *Cato Institute Tax and Budget Bulletin*, November 13, 2017, https://www.cato.org/publications/tax-budget-bulletin/low-income-housing-tax-credit-costly-complex-corruption-prone.

8 Ibid.

9 Howard Husock, "Don't Let CDCs Fool You," *City Journal*, Summer 2001, https://www.city-journal.org/html/don%E2%80%99t-let-cdcs-fool-you-12175.html.

10 Jill Khadduri, Carissa Climaco, and Kimberly Burnett, *What Happens to Low-Income Housing Tax Credit Properties at Year 15 and Beyond?*, special report prepared for United States Department of Housing and Urban Development, August 2012, https://www.huduser.gov/portal/publications/what_happens_lihtc_v2.pdf.

11 David P. Varady, Xinhao Wang, Yimei Wang, and Patrick Duhaney, "The Geographic Concentration of Housing Vouchers, Blacks, and Poverty Over

Time: A Study of Cincinnati, Ohio, USA," *Urban Research & Practice Journal* 3, no. 1 (February 2010): 39–62, https://doi.org/10.1080/17535060903534172.

12 Molly W. Metzger, "The Reconcentration of Poverty: Patterns of Housing Voucher Use, 2000 to 2008," *Housing Policy Debate Journal* 24, no. 3 (May 2014): 544–567, https://doi.org/10.1080/10511482.2013.876437.

13 Hanna Rosin, "American Murder Mystery," *Atlantic*, July/August 2008, https://www.theatlantic.com/magazine/archive/2008/07/american-murder-mystery/306872/.

14 Howard Husock, "Let's End Housing Vouchers," *City Journal*, Autumn 2000, https://www.city-journal.org/html/let%E2%80%99s-end-housing-vouchers-12152.html.

15 Peter Jamison, "D.C. Housed the Homeless in Upscale Apartments. It Hasn't Gone as Planned," *Washington Post*, April 16, 2019, https://www.washingtonpost.com/local/dc-politics/dc-housed-the-homeless-in-upscale-apartments-it-hasnt-gone-as-planned/2019/04/16/60c8ab9c-5648-11e9-8ef3-fbd41a2ce4d5_story.html.

16 Ingrid Gould Ellen, "Investigating the Relationship Between Housing Voucher Use and Crime," NYU Furman Center, March 2013, https://furmancenter.org/research/publication/investigating-the-relationship-between-housing-voucher-use-and-crime.

17 Michael C. Lens, Ingrid Gould Ellen, and Katherine O'Regan. "Do Vouchers Help Low Income Households Live in Safer Neighborhoods? Evidence on the Housing Choice Voucher Program," *Cityscape: A Journal of Policy Development and Research* 13, no. 3 (2011): 127–152, https://luskin.ucla.edu/sites/default/files/Lens%206%20Cityscape.pdf.

18 "Granada Gardens Apartments & Townhomes," Yelp, accessed March 9, 2021, https://www.yelp.com/biz/granada-gardens-apartments-and-townhomes-warrensville-heights.

19 Howard Husock, "How New York's Public Housing Fails the City's New Poor," *Manhattan Institute Issue Brief*, October 2017, https://media4.manhattan-institute.org/sites/default/files/IB-HH-1017-v2.pdf.

CHAPTER VIII: THE LEGACY OF LAWRENCE VEILLER:
ZONING OUT ZONES OF EMERGENCE

1 William A. Fischel, "Zoning Rules: The Economics of Land Use Regulation," Lincoln Institute of Land Policy, March 2015, https://www.lincolninst.edu/sites/default/files/pubfiles/zoning-rules-chp.pdf.

2 Roy Lubove, *The Progressives and the Slums: Tenement House Reform in New York City, 1900–1917* (Pittsburgh: University of Pittsburgh Press, 1962), 145.

3 "Housing Brevities," *American Architect*, no. 38, July 1920, https://books.google.com/books?id=VwVaAAAAYAAJ&pg=PA86. Veiller was also a key architect of a suggested state zoning law developed by the U.S. Department of Commerce in 1922, when future president Herbert Hoover served as its secretary. Zoning, however, is a local policy and federal suggestion did not mean universal change.

4 *A Standard State Zoning Enabling Act (Revised Edition)*, prepared by the Advisory Committee on Zoning and Secretary Herbert Hoover, U.S. Department of Commerce (Washington, D.C., 1926), https://www.govinfo. gov/content/pkg/GOVPUB-C1318b3b6e632119b6d94779f558b9d3873/pdf/ GOVPUB-C13-18b3b6e632119b6d94779f558b9d3873.pdf.

5 *Housing Betterment* 9, no. 1, February 1920.

6 Lawrence Veiller, *Model Housing Law* (New York: Russell Sage Foundation, 1920), 389.

7 Howard Husock, "Rediscovering the Three-Decker House," *National Affairs*, Winter 1990, https://www.nationalaffairs.com/storage/app/uploads/public/58e/ 1a4/982/58e1a4982867b814801907.pdf.

8 Robert C. Ellickson, "The Zoning Strait-Jacket: The Freezing of American Neighborhoods of Single-Family Houses," Yale Law School Public Law Research Paper, January 7, 2020, https://ssrn.com/abstract=3507803.

9 Ibid.

10 Ibid.

11 Ibid.

12 Mousumi Sarkar, *How American Homes Vary by the Year They Were Built*, Housing and Household Economic Statistics, working paper no. 2011-18, U.S. Census Bureau, June 2011, https://www.census.gov/content/dam/Census/ programs-surveys/ahs/working-papers/Housing-by-Year-Built.pdf.

13 David Schoenbrod, *Large Lot Zoning Note*, New York Law School, 1968, https://digitalcommons.nyls.edu/cgi/viewcontent. cgi?article=1241&context=fac_articles_chapters.

14 Alison Ring, *Town of Little Compton, Rhode Island, Comprehensive Plan*, adopted by the Little Compton Town Council, February 15, 2018, https:// www.littlecomptonri.org/Adopted%20and%20Approved%20Little%20 Compton%202018%20Comprehensive%20Plan%20Digital%20Copy%20 May%2018%202018.pdf.

15 The size of the average home built today (in the 2000s) is considerably larger than those built in earlier decades. It should be noted that older homes may have increased in size over the years due to additions and other renovation work. The median square footage of a single-family home built in the 1960s or earlier stands at 1,500 square feet today. In comparison, the median square footage of single-family homes built between 2005 and 2009 and between 2000 and 2004 stands today at 2,200 square feet and 2,100 square feet, respectively. Similarly, the median size of multifamily homes and mobile or manufactured homes has increased from a median of 800 square feet for these types of homes built in the 1960s or earlier to median sizes of 1,100 square feet and 1,200 square feet, respectively, for those built between 2005 and 2009. Author's note based on U.S. Census Bureau, "Characteristics of New Housing," https://www.census.gov/construction/chars/historical_data/.

16 "Characteristics of New Housing," United States Census Bureau, accessed November 10, 2020, https://www.census.gov/construction/chars/highlights. html.

17 Howard Husock, "Repairing the Ladder: Toward a New Housing Paradigm," *Reason Foundation*, July 1, 1996, https://reason.org/policy-study/repairing-the-ladder/.

18 *Why We Should Tackle Our Big Challenges at the Local Level*, American Enterprise Institute, February 2018, https://www.aei.org/wp-content/uploads/2018/02/Cox.Husock.2.pdf.

19 I thank my longtime neighbor Laura Hardy for coming to the polls at the last possible moment.

20 *"Not in My Backyard": Removing Barriers to Affordable Housing*, report to President Bush and Secretary Kemp by the Advisory Commission on Regulatory Barriers to Affordable Housing, July 8, 1991, https://www.huduser.gov/Publications/pdf/NotInMyBackyard_508.pdf.

21 William A. Fischel, "Zoning Rules: The Economics of Land Use Regulation," Lincoln Institute of Land Policy, March 2015, 24–25, https://www.lincolninst.edu/sites/default/files/pubfiles/zoning-rules-chp.pdf.

CHAPTER IX: MAXIMUM FEASIBLE OPPOSITION: THE LESSON OF MARIO CUOMO

1 Murray Kempton, "A Curious Politician," *New York Review of Books*, September 19, 1974, https://www.nybooks.com/articles/1974/09/19/a-curious-politician/.

2 Ibid.

3 Mario Cuomo, *Forest Hills Diary: The Crisis of Low-Income Housing* (New York: Random House, 1983).

4 Philip H. Rees, *Residential Patterns in American Cities: 1969* (University of Chicago Geography Research Papers) (Chicago: Committee on Geographical Studies, 1979).

5 Michael J. White, *American Neighborhoods and Residential Differentiation* (New York: Russell Sage Foundation, 1988), 27.

6 Herbert J. Gans, *The Levittowners: Ways of Life and Politics in a New Suburban Community* (New York: Pantheon Books, 1967), 171.

7 Anna Hardman and Yannis M. Ioannides, "Neighbors Income Distribution: Economic Segregation and Mixing in Urban Neighborhoods," *Journal of Housing Economics* 13 (2004): 368–338.

8 "Chapter 40 B Planning and Information," Mass.gov, accessed November 10, 2020, https://www.mass.gov/chapter-40-b-planning-and-information.

9 Sharon P. Krefetz, "The Impact and Evolution of the Massachusetts Comprehensive Permit and Zoning Appeals Act," *Western New England Law Review* 22, no. 2 (January 2001), https://digitalcommons.law.wne.edu/cgi/viewcontent.cgi?article=1182&context=lawreview.

10 "Massachusetts Population 1900–2019," Macrotrends, accessed November 10, 2020, https://www.macrotrends.net/states/massachusetts/population.

11 Eli Sherman, "A Breakdown of 40B Affordable Housing," *Patriot Ledger*, February 12, 2019, https://www.patriotledger.com/news/20190212/breakdown-of-40b-affordable-housing.

12 Ibid.

13 This section, including census-based income and demographic data, draws on the author's essay, "Housing as Busing," *City Journal*, Autumn 2009, https://www.city-journal.org/html/housing-busing-13237.html.

14 Liz Robbins, "Voters Roll Back Democratic Gains in New York Suburbs," *New York Times*, November 4, 2009, https://www.nytimes.com/2009/11/05/nyregion/05suburbs.html.

15 News 12 Staff, "Appeals Court Finds County Didn't Comply with Affordable Housing Settlement," News 12, April 28, 2017, http://westchester.news12.com/story/35281155/appeals-court-finds-county-didnt-comply-with-affordable-housing-settlement.

16 Sam Roberts, "Westchester Adds Housing to Desegregation Pact," *New York Times*, August 10, 2009, https://www.nytimes.com/2009/08/11/nyregion/11settle.html.

17 Jeffrey R. Kling, Jeffrey B. Liebman, Lawrence F. Katz, and Lisa Sanbonmatsu, "Moving to Opportunity and Tranquility: Neighborhood Effects on Adult Economic Self-Sufficiency and Health from a Randomized Housing Voucher Experiment," Faculty Research Working Papers Series, Harvard University Kennedy School of Government (August 2004).

18 Raj Chetty, Nathaniel Hendren, and Lawrence F. Katz, "The Effects of Exposure to Better Neighborhoods on Children: New Evidence from the Moving to Opportunity Experiment," *American Economic Review* 106, no. 4 (April 2016): 855–902.

19 Raj Chetty and Nathaniel Hendren, "The Impacts of Neighborhoods on Intergenerational Mobility: Childhood Exposure Effects and County-Level Estimates," *Quarterly Journal of Economics* 133, no. 3 (August 2018): 1107–1162.

20 Miriam Axel-Lute and Harold Simon, "Shelterforce Exclusive: Interview with HUD Secretary Julián Castro," *Shelterforce*, September 2015, https://shelterforce.org/2016/02/04/ishelterforce_i_exclusive_interview_with_hud_secretary_julian_castro2.

21 Barbara Sard and Douglas Rice, "Realizing the Housing Voucher Program's Potential to Enable Families to Move to Better Neighborhoods," Center on Budget and Policy Priorities, January 12, 2016, https://www.cbpp.org/research/housing/realizing-the-housing-voucher-programs-potential-to-enable-families-to-move-to.

22 Daniel Hertz, "Make Housing Vouchers an Entitlement—We Can Afford It," *City Commentary*, May 1, 2016, https://cityobservatory.org/make-housing-vouchers-an-entitlement-we-can-afford-it/.

23 Jeffrey R. Kling, Jeffrey B. Liebman, and Lawrence F. Katz, "Experimental Analysis of Neighborhood Effects," *Econometrica Journal*, no. 75 (January 2007): 83–119.

24 Kling, Liebman, Katz, and Sanbonmatsu, "Moving to Opportunity and Tranquility: Neighborhood Effects on Adult Economic Self-Sufficiency and Health from a Randomized Housing Voucher Experiment."

25 Donald J. Trump (@realDonaldTrump), "I am happy to inform all of the people living their Suburban Lifestyle Dream that you will no longer be

bothered or financially hurt by having low income housing built in your neighborhood," Twitter, July 29, 2020, 12:19 p.m., https://twitter.com/realdonaldtrump/status/1288509568578777088?s=12.

26 Sarah Wheeler, "Julian Castro on Trump's AFFH Tweet: 'It's a Naked Ploy to Drum Up Racial Fears and White Resentment,'" HousingWire, July 31, 2020, https://www.housingwire.com/articles/julian-castro-on-trumps-affh-tweet-its-a-naked-ploy-to-drum-up-racial-fears-and-white-resentment/.

27 Ingrid Gould Ellen, "What Do We Know About Housing Choice Vouchers?" NYU Furman Center, August 14, 2017, https://furmancenter.org/files/fact-sheets/HousingChoiceVouchers_WorkingPaper_IngridGouldEllen_14AUG2017.pdf.

28 Robert D. Putnam, "E Pluribus Unum: Diversity and Community in the Twenty-First Century: The 2006 Johan Skytte Prize Lecture," *Scandinavian Political Studies Journal* 30, no. 2 (2007): 137–174.

CHAPTER X: SLUMS OF HOPE

1 "Millennium Development Goals and Beyond 2015: Goal 7: Ensure Environmental Sustainability," United Nations, accessed November 10, 2020, https://www.un.org/millenniumgoals/environ.shtml.

2 United Nations Human Settlement Program, *The Challenge of Slums: Global Report on Human Settlements*, Earthscan, London and Sterling, VA, 2003, https://www.un.org/ruleoflaw/files/Challenge%20of%20Slums.pdf.

3 Mike Davis, *Planet of Slums* (London and New York: Verso, 2006), 19.

4 Wallace Stegner, "Pop Goes the Alley Cat," in *Collected Stories of Wallace Stegner* (New York: Random House, 1989), 253.

5 Robert Neuwirth, *Shadow Cities: A Billion Squatters, a New Urban World* (London and New York: Routledge, 2005), 10.

6 In Howard Husock, "Slums of Hope," *City Journal*, Winter 2009.

7 Buk-Swienty, Preface, XV.

8 Bonnie Yochelson and Daniel Czitrom, *Rediscovering Jacob Riis: Exposure Journalism and Photography in Turn-of-the-Century New York* (University of Chicago Press, 2007), 116.

9 "A Flourishing Slum," *The Economist*, December 22, 2007.

10 Jane Jacobs, *The Economy of Cities* (New York: Vintage Books, 1970), 120–121.

11 Based on author's interview.

12 Ibid.

13 Hernando de Soto, *The Mystery of Capital* (New York: Basic Books, 2000), 18.

14 Jordana Barton, Emily Ryder Perlmeter, Elizabeth Sobel Blum, and Raquel R. Marquez, *Las Colonias in the 21st Century: Progress Along the Texas-Mexico Border*, report prepared for the Federal Reserve Bank of Dallas, April 2015, https://www.dallasfed.org/~/media/documents/cd/pubs/lascolonias.pdf.

15 Ibid.

16 Sophie Quinton, "States Contend with 'The Underbelly of American Real Estate,'" *Stateline News Service*, June 1, 2016, https://www.pewtrusts.org/en/

research-and-analysis/blogs/stateline/2016/06/01/states-contend-with-the-underbelly-of-real-estate.

17 Peter Ward, Cecilia Giusti, and Flavio de Souza, "Colonia Land and Housing Market Performance and the Impact of Lot Title Regularization in Texas," *Urban Studies* 41, no. 13 (December 2004): 2621–2646, https://www.researchgate.net/publication/248973600_Colonia_Land_and_Housing_Market_Performance_and_the_Impact_of_Lot_Title_Regularization_in_Texas.

18 "CDC Spotlight: A Holistic Approach to Housing in Brownsville," *Texas Housers*, December 3, 2015, https://texashousers.org/2015/12/03/cdc-spotlight-a-holistic-approach-to-housing-in-brownsville/.

19 Ibid.

CHAPTER XI: UNREFORMING HOUSING

1 "Moving to Work," Housing Authority of the County of San Bernardino, accessed November 10, 2020, http://www.hacsb.com/about-hacsb/moving-to-work.

2 *Hearing: Evaluating How HUDs Moving-to-Work Program Benefits Public and Assisted Housing Residents*, House Subcommittee on Housing and Insurance, Washington, D.C., June 26, 2013.

3 Housing Authority of San Bernardino, *Moving to Work: Annual Report* (California, 2019), 24, https://hacsb.com/moving-to-work/.

4 Howard Husock, "Ending NYCHA's Dependence Trap: Making Better Use of New York's Public Housing," Manhattan Institute, September 19, 2019, https://www.manhattan-institute.org/making-nycha-more-efficient.

5 "The U.S. Has National Shortage of More Than 7.2 Million Affordable & Available Rental Homes for Families Most in Need," National Low Income Housing Coalition, May 13, 2018, https://nlihc.org/news/us-has-national-shortage-more-72-million-affordable-available-rental-homes-families-most-need.

6 "America's Rental Housing 2020," Joint Center for Housing Studies of Harvard University, accessed November 10, 2020, https://www.jchs.harvard.edu/americas-rental-housing-2020. "Despite slowing demand and the continued strength of new construction, rental markets in the U.S. remain extremely tight. Vacancy rates are at decades-long lows, pushing up rents far faster than incomes. Both the number and share of cost-burdened renters are again on the rise, especially among middle-income households."

7 Emily Badger and Quoctrung Bui, "Cities Start to Question an American Ideal: A House with a Yard in Every Lot," *New York Times*, June 18, 2019, https://www.nytimes.com/interactive/2019/06/18/upshot/cities-across-america-question-single-family-zoning.html.

8 Author's notes.

9 Howard Husock, "Minneapolis: Before the Storm," *City Journal*, August 25, 2020, https://www.city-journal.org/minneapolis-2040-plan.

10 Indeed, when one looks at relatively affluent parts of the city, African

Americans do not appear to be excluded. In Linden Hills, 4.3 percent of the population is African American, not wildly out of line when considering that only 7.4 percent of the population of the metropolitan area is African American. In the Victory neighborhood, as well, we see an overlap between an affluent population and African American households: In a neighborhood in which 40 percent are among the city's highest-income earners, some 18 percent of households are African American.

11 Husock, *City Journal.*

12 "City of Shorewood: Zoning Districts," Shorewood Minnesota, accessed November 10, 2020, http://ci.shorewood.mn.us/zoning%20map.pdf.

13 Daniel G. Parolek, *Missing Middle Housing Thinking Big and Building Small to Respond to Today's Housing Crisis* (New York: Island Press, 2020).

14 "Missing Middle Housing," Missing Middle Housing, accessed November 10, 2020, https://missingmiddlehousing.com/.

15 Janice Bitters, "San Jose: Permits for 'Granny Units' Spiked Last Year, but 2020 May Be Bigger," *San Jose Spotlight,* January 20, 2020, https://sanjosespotlight.com/san-jose-permits-for-granny-units-spiked-last-year-but-2020-may-be-bigger/. "Last year was a big year for accessory dwelling units—or 'granny units'—in San Jose, where the number of people seeking to build the little backyard homes nearly doubled from 2018, and the number permitted to start construction grew even faster. Recent San Jose data shows that 695 applications for new ADUs were received by the city in 2019, compared to 350 the year before. Meanwhile, 416 ADU projects were granted permits to move forward last year, which is more than twice the number of permits issued in 2018."

INDEX